Understanding Co-dependency

Sharon Wegscheider-Cruse, M.A.
Joseph R. Cruse, M.D.

Health Communications, Inc.
Deerfield Beach, Florida

Sharon Wegscheider-Cruse, M.A., and
Joseph R. Cruse, M.D.
ONSITE Training & Consulting, Inc.
2820 West Main
Rapid City, South Dakota 57702

Library of Congress Cataloging-in-Publication Data

Wegscheider-Cruse, Sharon
   Understanding co-dependency / by Sharon Wegscheider-
   Cruse and Joseph R. Cruse.
     p.   cm.
   Includes bibliographical references.
   ISBN 1-55874-077-5
   1. Co-dependence (Psychology)   I. Cruse, Joseph R.
II. Title.
RC569.5.C63W34   1990   89-29517
616.86—dc20   CIP

Publisher: Health Communications, Inc.
         3201 S.W. 15th Street
         Deerfield Beach, Florida 33442

*Dedicated to the pioneers
in the field of addictive disease —
those who make paths —
not just follow them . . .*

Dear Reader,

Co-dependency has been a confusing term for so many. This book is an attempt to simplify and offer clarity. It is our hope that when you are finished, you will understand a framework of this illness that will be helpful to you. . . .

CONTENTS

INTRODUCTION

During the past few years, many books have been written about co-dependency, and it's been the subject of countless lectures and workshops. The intent has been to bring hope and healing to hurting people.

When such important new information becomes widely known so rapidly, an irreversible movement is formed.

In the last ten years, there have been several singularly powerful events in the field of addictive disease.

1. Acceptance of the process of intervention to help an alcoholic/addict get to the point of accepting treatment.
2. Acceptance of the fact that addiction is a family disease and all members need help.
3. The standard use of both in-patient and out-patient programs for both the alcoholic/addict and family members.
4. The explosion of the Adult Children movement. This refers to children of alcoholics.
5. The expansion of Adult Children of Alcoholics to Adult Children from any painful family system.

6. An awareness, on a large scale, of the word co-dependency and a new movement called the co-dependency field.

There are countless theories, concepts and ideas, which
results in a confused . . .

- Public
- Media
- Treatment field.

In an effort to understand the phenomenon of co-dependency, many authors have instead complicated the issue with their own specific ideas and interpretations. However, an overload of specifics can increase confusion
unless we have a framework to understand the whole.

> *An overload of specifics can increase confusion un-
> less we have a framework to understand the whole.*

It takes the work of many people coming from many
directions to put together an understanding of a complicated disease. Together we are well on the way to that
understanding.

Some of us have concentrated on the *process* in the individual's brain. Others have concentrated on the *Person* and
the development stages and events that occur in their lives.
Others have concentrated on the *society* or *environment* in
which the disease occurs. Most are learning to deal with
the disease and are discovering and sharing solutions and
treatment aspects of all the above.

There are three dimensions we can study in looking at
co-dependency.

1. The *person* — who gets co-dependency?
2. The *process* — the disease itself.
3. The *planet* — environment.

The *person* who gets or has the disease is a person who

is disabled. This person is hurting and afflicted with self-defeating behaviors which are a result of their internalized emotional pain.

The *process:* The disease is an accumulation of thoughts, feelings and behaviors that rest in the brain. This is the process that needs to be treated.

The *planet* refers to all the person's relationships. Many co-dependents in early life were involved in toxic relationships and have not learned, as adults, to form healthy connections. Their aftercare plan will be to address all their relationships.

Some criticism of the co-dependency movement is that it is too general, applies to everyone and therefore loses its meaning. This criticism is understandable and only adds to the existing confusion. However, in reality the disease of co-dependency is the result of chemical responses or changes in the brain brought on by very specific behaviors.

Sight and hearing have their own pathways. Memory and learning have their own system. Knowledge uses the back areas of the brain while memory uses the front and middle portions of the brain (Resnak 1988).

Neuroscience has mapped out many complex behaviors such as eating and drinking. Their chemical basis and their functioning also have been described and have been classed as motivational behaviors. Mood-altering behaviors are also motivational behaviors.

These behaviors have a tendency to become compulsive and repetitive. They increase in frequency, duration, intensity and variety because we develop a tolerance to their original benefits. Eventually, most compulsive mood-changing behaviors and mood-changing substances become ingrained and *disabling.* Whenever a body/mind/spirit becomes disabled by one process or another, the process can then be classed as a disease and will remain so, even in the face of adverse consequences. We see it often in eating disorders, nicotine addiction and alcoholism.

When a person moves from choice to powerlessness and when the self-defeating behavior becomes disabling because of tolerance, we can say the person has developed the disease of co-dependency.

Co-dependents developed survival roles to help them get through troubled childhoods. Some outlasted and out-grew their childhood survival roles and behaviors; others attended support groups and were able to make significant self-nurturing changes. But many who developed co-dependency tended to repeat the self-defeating behaviors they had used as children. As adults they became trapped in their own compulsions, giving up one behavior only to turn to another substance or behavior. They gave up alcohol, only to start marathon running. They gave up nicotine and began to compulsively eat sugar. They gave up caretaking and began workaholism.

What is happening is that the old pain of childhood keeps triggering a need for substances or behavior to bring some relief to the co-dependent and the cycle keeps repeating itself. This is the person who has become disabled and needs treatment.

It becomes the responsibility of the professional to learn to assess, diagnose and treat according to the symptomatology presented.

The person who simply needs to go to a 12-Step support group or read a daily meditation book is not the same person who needs to be in an inpatient treatment program to address clinically diagnosable, self-defeating avoidant behavior, nicotine addiction and disabling grief.

Learning more about the specifics of co-dependency contains both the good news and the bad news. We are able to see that many of our patients are "weller" than previously thought and many are "sicker." And many requiring help for other mental illnesses are migrating into co-dependency self-help groups and treatment programs. Treatment programs need to sort them out and give them the help that they require. We know that co-dependency is an illness that has many stages and levels, which will be further described as we go along.

The press, the media and the authors have contributed to a fair amount of confusion about this word. If I had a magic wand, we would drop the word altogether and refer to a much clearer description of what is happening. We would prefer to call co-dependency *co-existing dependencies*. This would describe more accurately what we see in the individuals we treat.

As we learn to understand the disease, it becomes easier to . . .

1. Know which author to read for what purposes.
2. Design treatment plans and recovery routes (people are unique and different but the disease process is similar).
3. Measure outcomes and results of treatment.
4. Set standards of accountability.
5. Ensure safety and quality for each patient and client.

For the past 10 to 15 years, authors have been describing what they thought co-dependency was all about. Some approaches were scientific, some popular for the mass media and some treatment-focused.

As we look at a model that includes the person, the disease process and the environment, we can see the contributions of each of the authors and how their perspectives contribute to the whole. Looking at each author's work reduces confusion and increases understanding.

We have listed many of the current authors and what we see as their major areas of focus in their writings. We hope the list on the following pages will be useful for you.

Examples Of Writings And Theories Of Co-dependency

The Person

Personality Theory — Development Theory

1. Claudia Black, *Children of Alcoholics*
2. Timmen Cermak, *Post-Traumatic Stress Narcissism Antithesis*

   3. C. Robert Cloninger, *Genetic Personality Dimensions*
   4. Erik Erikson, *Stages of Development*
   5. Rokelle Lerner, *Arrested Development*
   6. Pia Mellody, *The Inner Child*
   7. Jane Middelton-Moz, *Delayed Stress Syndrome*
   8. Sondra Smalley, *Learned Painful Beliefs and Behaviors*
   9. Robert Subby, *Delayed Identity Formation*
  10. Charles Whitfield, *The Inner Child*

The Disease Process

Reinforcement Theory — Addiction Theory

Brain Events

   1. Floyd Bloom, *Neurochemistry*
   2. Joseph Cruse, Sharon Wegscheider-Cruse, *Brain Reward Systems/Tolerance*
   3. Max Schneider, *Nicotine Addiction*
   4. B. F. Skinner, *Learning Stimulus-Response Response-Stimulus*
   5. Boris Tabakoff, *Tolerance*
   6. Arnold Washton, *Addictive Process*
   7. Mary Lee Zawadski, *Internal Needs — External Needs*
   8. All authors addressing specific behaviors, such as sexual acting out, gambling, excessive exercise, eating disorders, excessive control and caretaking, e.g., Terry Kellogg, *Sexual Compulsivity.*

Life Events

   1. Robert Ackerman, Susan Pickering, *Women and Relationships*
   2. Melody Beattie, *Relationships*
   3. John Bradshaw, *Toxic Shame*
   4. Ralph Earle, *Loneliness*
   5. Marilyn Mason, *Shame — Guilt*
   6. Max Schneider, *Medical Complications of Co-dependency*
   7. Robert Subby, *Intimacy*

The Environment

Anthropological-Systems Theory

1. Robert Ackerman, *Adult Children of Alcoholics*
2. Philip Diaz and Pat O'Gorman, *Families and Parenting*
3. John and Linda Friel, *Oppressive Family Systems*
4. Terry Gorski, *Chemically Dependent Family Systems*
5. Carl Jung, *Collective Subconscious*
6. John Neikirk, *The Workplace*
7. Virginia Satir, *Family Systems*
8. Anne Wilson Schaef, *Addictive Society*
9. Sharon Wegscheider-Cruse, *Painful Family Systems*

Consensus On Co-dependency

If we read the works of the many authors in the field of co-dependency and recovery, we begin to notice something very interesting. Second writings from each of the authors seem to be closer to one another than were their first writings. In effect, these writings are beginning to merge toward a coherent voice (Ackerman 1989, Cermak 1988, Cruse 1989, Gorski 1989, Washton 1989, Whitfield 1990, Subby 1990). This probably happens because the authors are adjusting their particular perspectives and broadening their missions.

In spite of this there are still some problems in communication. The way these problems operate can best be described by using the parable of the blind men and the elephant. In this story, each of the blind men was asked to describe the part of the elephant directly in front of him. Each gave an accurate description but each description was totally different. None of them came up with the concept of an elephant, although each of their descriptions was accurate. Perhaps if those of us working on co-dependency could remove our blindfolds, we could converge even more in our individual searches.

In September, 1989, 22 such individuals gathered to-gether in Scottsdale, Arizona, and came up with a consen-sus description or definition of co-dependency. It was . . .

Co-dependency is a pattern of painful dependency on com-pulsive behaviors and on approval from others in an attempt to find safety, self-worth and identity. Recovery is possible.

In the next chapter, we would like to share with you the model we have developed in our co-dependency treatment program.

Premise: The Co-dependency Trap

So often we hear co-dependents say:

1. Why do I keep doing the same things over and over?
2. Why can't I stop thinking about certain things?
3. If I look so good, why do I feel so bad?
4. Why can't I stop hurting myself with drugs, ciga-rettes, people, food, alcohol, gambling, etc.?

These answers are best found in understanding the brain. It is this organ with which we are dealing when we try to understand and treat co-dependency.

To completely understand the dynamics of co-dependency, we need to understand a new science. This science has many different names, such as *neuro-psychology, psycho-neuro biology* or *neuro-chemistry*.

Jon Franklin, Pulitzer Prize-winning author on describing brain function, says simply:

The basis of this new discipline is the perception that human thought, emotion and behavior results from the inner play of molecules across the surface of brain cells.

The brain provides a model of function and disease — a paradigm. Thomas Kuhn gives importance to the term paradigm in his book *The Structure of Scientific Revolutions* when he says, "Without commitment to a paradigm (model), there can be no science."

We have found it necessary when designing a treatment program for co-dependency that a scientific model be established for the purposes of providing us, our patients, our staff and our colleagues with the necessary degree of specificity, accountability and predictability.

Is Co-dependency A Brain Disorder?

Immediately the reader may feel some discomfort with the concepts of mental illness or co-dependency as being basically a brain disorder. Those of you who were trained in the '50s to '70s are familiar with the conflict that exists between the scientific community and the adaptive or humanistic community. The division between these disciplines is likened to the differences in the disciplines between Eastern and Western medicine.

Those in the West direct their efforts toward precise cause and effect, signs and symptoms and continual self-evaluation. There tends to be an appreciation of the chronology of events, staging and classifications. Whereas, in the East, the new brain information supports much of what they have known for centuries through the practice of healing, meditation and prayer. In this country we have seen the mainstream of scientific concern and 12-Step programs merge closer. It seems as though the Nature versus Nurture controversy is becoming more Nature plus Nurture.

Dr. Joseph T. Quail of Johns Hopkins School of Medicine states:

> With advances in research on the brain over the last 15 years, we have now reached the point that neuroscience can justifiably be considered the biomedical foundation of psychiatry.

In no other area is this information as easily understood as it is in learning to understand co-dependency.

In co-dependency, it is the interaction between one's own manufactured "brain chemicals" (having to do with our reinforcement center) and one's behavior that stimulates the brain to establish compulsive and addictive behavior processes.

Many have thought that co-dependency has been due to life's problems, such as living with an alcoholic or addict, having low self-worth, being from an alcoholic family, etc. But it's the other way around. Because we have a brain that gives us an excessive rush, we get into self-defeating behaviors that keep the rush coming (co-dependency).

What Is A Rush?

A "rush" needs to be explained here. Some are exhilarating and some are quieting. All involve a change of mood. Examples would be:

Chemical	Behavior	Produces
dopamine	running	excitement
	gambling	excitement
	hang-gliding	excitement
serotonin	overeating	calm-comfort
	relationship dependency	comfort
norepinephrine	workaholism	power-control
	caretaking	power-control

These are only examples. There are many chemicals and behaviors being studied.

It is important to know that we manipulate our moods — our highs and our lows — by our ingestion of chemicals from the outside (alcohol, drugs, nicotine or sugar). We do the same thing when we engage in selected, repetitive behaviors that release our inner chemicals.

The living problems, listed above, are *results* of having the disease of co-dependency *not* the *cause*.

With this knowledge, the patients, the staff, the referrents all understand co-dependency treatment. The primary treatment focus is to address the person and the person's brain processes (distorted thoughts, feelings and behaviors). The need for aftercare is to address the issues in the person's life that have been hurt by the brain disease (relationships, self-worth and medical complications).

Knowing such specifics in treating co-dependency has helped us in many ways and forced us to develop new tools and better methods in confronting denial, arresting compulsion and creating an atmosphere which will allow our patients the most freedom to access their emotional life.

Using traditional modalities of group dynamics, Gestalt, psychodrama and rage reduction, we have added formalized individual and group sculptures to specifically address co-dependency issues. These experiential methods are interwoven with the 12 Steps, brain education, relationship exercises, etc. We have designed a text that will train therapists in this style of treatment. It's called *"Experiential Therapy for Co-dependency."*

The Co-dependency Trap

When we can no longer attach what we feel to the event that caused it, we have a kind of free-floating depression or anxiety. There is a sense of discomfort, a sense of uneasiness inside. Some describe it as a panic in the chest. Others describe it as literally a pain in their stomach. Some just feel like the end is coming, that they or the world is going to fall apart, a sense of impending doom.

The abscess is growing and the chronic pain becomes tiresome. When we find a medicating substance or behavior that works, it works through a specific area, the *ventral tegmentum* (Bozarth 1987), in the brain which comes in the form of reward or relief. We are signaling for help. "I need reward." "I need relief." "I need to change my internal environment." "I need to *feel* better." Many substances and many compulsive behaviors trigger our reward/relief/novelty center for temporary easing of the discomfort.

We each seek those particular compulsive medicators that work best for us. Based on our genetic makeup, based on our environmental learnings and present circumstances, based on the amount and newness of the relief or reward, compulsive medicators are used with increasing frequency, increasing duration, increasing intensity and increasing variety. These increases are necessary because we quickly develop tolerance, that is, we become accustomed to our medicators. We need ever-increasing doses of frequency, duration, intensity and variety to keep our medicators working. Usually it's the excessive use of our medicators that causes the disability that results from our co-dependency.

For those that are going to become alcohol or chemically dependent, a certain genetic makeup needs to be present. But they, too, have an underlying craving for reward, relief or novelty, all of which temporarily decrease the emotional pain.

Components Present For Chemical Dependency

There are three components to chemical dependency:

1. Genes that result in a person being susceptible (the *person*).
2. An agent that can cause the disease, such as alcohol or drugs (the *process*).
3. There must be a permissive or even a promotive environment or society for the person and the agent to get together (the *planet*).

Perhaps the alcoholism in your family is three generations back, perhaps it was the last generation. Either way, you can have the genes for chemical dependency. About 10 to 20 percent of adults in the United States have those genes that give them a particular kind of chemical relief from "outside" chemicals. A lot of people experiment and even overuse and misuse drugs and alcohol. For 10 to 20 percent of the population, drugs and alcohol provide some degree of special relief for the pain of an emotional abscess.

The chemicals that work from the outside on our brain are certain legal and illegal drugs — alcohol, nicotine and, perhaps, caffeine and sugar.

Among the chemicals that work from the outside there are distinct differences. Nicotine, for example, is so reinforcing and works so fast and so subtly that anyone can become nicotine addicted and stay addicted for years and years, even after he or she stops smoking. On the other hand, someone has to have the proper genetic makeup before he or she will become addicted to alcohol (Ashton 1987).

As yet we don't know how sugar addiction occurs, whether it is like alcohol addiction in that people are genetically predisposed to become addicted or not, but we do know that, for some people, sugar is an addictive mood-changing substance.

So it appears that only certain people are likely to become addicted to alcohol and certain drugs but it is possible for anyone to become addicted to nicotine and other kinds of drugs.

Drugs, alcohol, nicotine, caffeine and sugar have varying powers to quiet the craving that has been triggered by emotional pain but all are effective to some degree or another.

Behavioral Addiction

What happens to the 80 to 90 percent of the population who don't have the genes that make such outside chemicals, such as alcohol, work? If they have lived in painful kinds of situations and if they have developed similar kinds of emotional abscesses, how do they cope? What we are now learning about the chemistry of the brain is helpful in understanding how they cope.

Today we know that we can become intoxicated and toxic with our own internal chemicals, set off by behavior. We know we can also become "addicts" to and through our own behavior that can set off certain chemicals which satisfy our craving for relief.

The medicating behaviors that we see most often are:

- Workaholism
- Compulsive eating, which is different from sugar addiction
- Compulsive controlling of eating, such as anorexia, a highly medicating behavior
- Compulsive caretaking and controlling others
- Seduction
- Sexual acting out

- Spending and gambling
- Excessive exercise
- What we term "guru-chasing."

This last medicating behavior is seen in people trying to recover from adult child issues who are continually medicating these issues by chasing the newest "it," following the latest method of recovery, going to four or more different kinds of groups, going to numerous conferences, reading all the books and getting all the tapes, trying to find something that is going to fix them and take care of them, once and for all.

Chasing only temporarily medicates issues and pain. For example, consider the Adult Child from an alcoholic family who compulsively keeps trying to get weller and weller and who says, "I've been doing it all for two years and nothing's any better!" In fact, all they've been doing is medicating but not opening and working through the emotional abscess.

Inside chemicals stimulated by compulsive behaviors or outside chemicals taken inside will temporarily quiet them but then both kinds of medicators require repeating with increasing frequency, duration, amount and variety to overcome tolerance. In this way, individuals become addicted to, or dependent on, their behaviors or substances or a combination of behaviors or substances. Certainly it's a rare individual who is only a workaholic or an alcoholic or only a nicotine addict or only has an eating disorder. Scratch the paint off a substance abuser and you find a "behavioral" abuser. Most individuals have many Co-existing Dependencies.

Certainly it's a rare individual who is only a workaholic or an alcoholic or only a nicotine addict or only has an eating disorder. Scratch the paint off a substance abuser and you find a "behavioral" abuser. Most individuals have many Co-existing Dependencies.

What happens after every high or rush? The result of medicating is called the "high." Whether it comes in a package of novelty, reward or relief, it's still a high. And what do we know happens after every high? You crash. And you say to yourself . . .

"Damn it, I did it again! I didn't mean to."

"This time I meant to really, really manage the way I work in my job."

"This time I really, really meant to abstain, be honest and committed and faithful."

"This time I really, really meant to just live some sort of a simple life for a while and I found myself signing up for three more workshops."

"I didn't mean to eat that Twinkie."

"I didn't mean to have another drink."

"I didn't intend to have a cigarette on the way home from the program."

This is negative reinforcement and it's filled with disgust. We don't like ourselves and we reinforce our own shame as our self-worth plummets and our abscess grows.

There comes a time to say, "I'm finished with it!" There comes a time when it is obvious that we must get rid of all the feelings about it. That's what treatment is for . . . to get rid of it. To work through the abscess, not on the abscess.

Many people who are still struggling have worked on the same issues 15 times or more. "I want to keep working on this issue." "I found one more piece of this issue." Such head talk is making a commitment to shame and to staying in the pathology, rather than going through it or letting it go and making a commitment not to go back to the same issue. We reinforce our shame when we go back and drag ourselves through it one more time. Sometimes, in a way, it's easier than recovery.

When you recover, you have a lot of new responsibilities. And you've a lot of things to do. Intimacy is possible but now there also are new possibilities for failure because also there are so many options open to you. Many people are really afraid to recover and this is why they

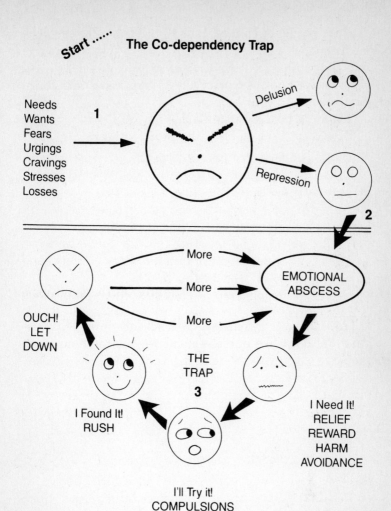

Figure 1.1 Co-dependency: Reinforcement Theory.

keep finding one more problem to work on. Familiar pain can be comfortable and can be a means of bonding with people and obtaining acceptance. Misery loves company. Okay, so we crashed and we feel disgusted with ourselves. Once more we feel guilty. And for many of us, we feel just plain stupid. We feed the emotional abscess so it gets bigger. And the bigger it gets, the more relief we crave.

Just as we develop a tolerance to the effects of chemicals, we develop a tolerance to the effects of behavior. Now it isn't just one promotion, I need two promotions and it's got to be better. It isn't just getting a raise, it's getting a big raise and some public recognition.

For the person who is acting out, it's got to be more (frequency) and more (duration) and more (variety) and more (intensity) to overcome tolerance.

This is the whole trap of co-dependency. The vicious one-way circle is a trap, ending in depression, isolation, institutions and, even, death.

Personality And The Progression Into Disease

In 1976 after studying many families, it was easy to see that disabled families fall into patterns of self-defeating behavior that Sharon titled The Enabler, Family Hero, Scapegoat, Lost Child and Mascot.

Family Hero

He or she provides the moments of hope and pride that the family desperately needs. The hero tries to bring self-worth to the family. To the outside world the hero looks great but on the inside the hero feels miserable. Inadequacy, loneliness and fatigue contribute to feelings of worthlessness and of being overwhelmed.

Scapegoat

He or she withdraws from the family. Scapegoats try to spend more and more time physically away from the family, yet take with them a hunger for belonging and anger because they do not belong at home. This need for belonging and the pain of anger often leads the scapegoat to painful peer groups and experimentation with chemicals. Chemical dependency, negative behavior and suicide are often escapes for the hurting person.

Lost Child

Lost children adapt. They become loners, trying to survive a painful environment. In the midst of family chaos they withdraw into themselves. This child is often forgotten to the degree of neglect. As these children build walls of isolation, they miss out on how to develop relationships. They suffer from intense loneliness.

Mascots

Mascots are filled with fear (of being left out) and loneliness (they are rarely taken seriously by the family). To try to become included, mascots turn to teasing, joking or any agitating behavior to attract attention to themselves. Mascots may act cute or helpless, interrupt or act "crazy" but are very hard to ignore.

These roles are clearly explained in Sharon's book *Another Chance: Hope and Help for the Alcoholic Family*.

The roles proved to be useful to both the layperson and also to those professionals working with alcoholic families. Over the years, the roles become ingrained in work with all painful families, not just the alcoholic family. Many therapists, school and treatment programs developed their approach to helping families by using the roles. The film and video *The Family Trap*, which gives Sharon's philosophy about the roles, has become a classic in treatment programs.

However, many in the scientific community, while recognizing the value of the roles, wanted to know *why* they were so accurate and *how* identifying with them helped an individual.

These questions remained unanswered until the work of C. Robert Cloninger (1987) became known. Cloninger has described three dimensions of the personality seen in chemically dependent individuals. These are the same dimensions we have clearly seen in many co-dependents. They are:

1. Reward Dependence
2. Novelty Seeking
3. Harm Avoidance

One person may become highly active searching for reward and validation, which is typical of the Reward

Dependent person. Another may overuse their personality trait of Novelty Seeking, the living-on-the-edge kind of person. Then we have a personality dimension for Harm Avoidance. These dimensions have been determined before you were ever born.

The Novelty Seeker is the kind of person who seeks excitement and is never satisfied. The Novelty Seeker likes to live with crisis and adventure.

The Harm Avoidant person likes to keep things the same. Just don't rock the boat. Keep it the same. He or she likes things to be easy, likes to appear normal to the outside world, takes no risks and is always on guard to avoid conflict and punishment.

The Reward Dependent, as the name implies, seeks rewards and is always ready to "grab for the ring" or prize. They control constantly in an attempt to maintain the status quo. Self-worth depends on accomplishment, position, possessions (including people) and power. This trait is exemplified by workaholics. As reward dependents, they frenetically seek the pat on the back. They need to have the approval of others.

All of us have some of these inherited traits. When these traits work for us, they grow into balanced, mature and flexible behaviors that we can use.

Problems come when we exaggerate our normal personality patterns into a disorder. For example, the person who seeks excitement and drama, who is never satisfied, lives on the edge and becomes preoccupied with self as a means of coping with stress and emotional pain, crosses a fine line from balanced and flexible novelty-seeking to exaggerated novelty-seeking.

Learning about these three dimensions of the personality helped us to understand further the family roles first pointed out by Sharon.

The Novelty Seeker (Cloninger 1987) can become a clinical narcissist, a borderline personality or a histrionic. This type of person, as a child, might be evident as the Scapegoat or Mascot (Wegscheider-Cruse 1976).

The exaggerated Harm Avoidant (Cloninger 1987) tends to become The Enabler or Lost Child (Wegscheider-Cruse 1976) and is likely to become clinically diagnosed as having an avoidant personality disorder, progressing at times to a schizoid (isolated) personality disorder. He or she also may be clinically depressed.

The Reward Dependent person (Cloninger 1987) becomes obsessive-compulsive or passive-aggressive. We might see this person in the family as the Family Hero or The Enabler (Wegscheider-Cruse 1976).

**Co-dependent And Chemical Dependent
Personality Dimensions**

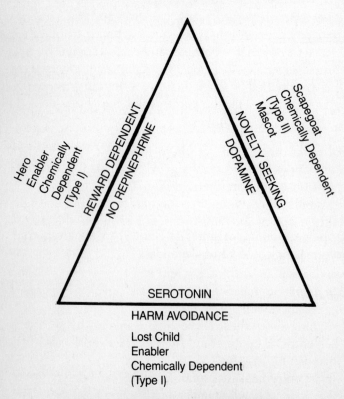

**Figure 2.1. Inherited Personality Dimensions
(Cloninger, modified).**

What continually reinforces each personality pattern is the release of relief or reward brain chemicals.

The Mascot and the Scapegoat in the family are often Novelty Seekers. Both the Family Hero and the Lost Child can become enablers, quite likely to marry alcoholics. When a Harm Avoidant spouse marries an alcoholic, it is likely that it is a Harm Avoidant marrying a Novelty Seeker. These two play off each other's pathology.

One of the things that occurs is that Novelty Seekers get "high" on their own internal chemicals. The reason they exaggerate this dimension of their personality and take risks, make sudden changes and create crises over and over again is that they can get chemically high on it, with an effect similar to that produced by alcohol or drugs. We know that Novelty Seekers, through this behavior, release their own internal dopamine, a brain chemical used to transmit "high" messages throughout our bodies.

Reward Dependent workaholics are probably releasing their own norepinephrine (adrenaline). Good workaholics are probably releasing both norepinephrine and dopamine. They're staying as medicated as a person smoking dope.

Harm Avoidant individuals who go to their rooms and hide out watching TV, eating potato chips and purging are releasing their own serotonin, a built-in tranquilizer we all have.

This information helps us understand the roles and why they are so important. But could it mean, then, that everyone is or could be co-dependent?

Not at all!

Co-dependency represents a collection of disabling compulsions accompanied by delusion and emotional repression and is the first step in the progression from health to disease. This first step occurs when we cross a line from balanced and flexible traits and dimensions to rigid and exaggerated traits and dimensions.

There is a point where we progress from the normal "traits" we all have and exaggerate those traits into a rigid, self-defeating pattern.

The work of Theodore Millon (1985-87) suggests that the inherited aspects of our personalities are influenced by prenatal and natal factors to which are added experiences and learnings as we grow. Theoretically, we all should end up with a normal personality that faces adversity and recovers time and time again.

What Is Mental Illness?

Millon and others consider that mental illnesses are deviations from the normal personality traits. Exaggeration of one set of traits gives rise to one type of personality disorder or mental illness, while exaggeration of another set of traits results in another type of mental illness or personality disorder. Others think that mental illnesses are each distinct and believe that an outside process has intruded upon a person's thinking, feeling and behaving. (This view is certainly correct for certain infections that cause mental confusion, impulsive behavior, etc.)

It appears to us that co-dependency is an exaggeration of normal personality traits to a degree that a person becomes disabled (disease of co-dependency). Although Millon suggests that personality disorders result from exaggerated personality traits, we see co-dependency as a "pre-personality disorder." The difference we see thus far is a matter of degree and reversibility. Co-dependency does not seem to be as restricting or ingrained as are the actual personality disorders.

Co-dependency can be as severe and disabling as the personality disorders but co-dependents seem to have more recovery resources and choices available to them, whether they know it or not. Many times our treatment succeeds primarily in showing them that they have such choices and resources. Persons with personality disorders seem to have less access to their resources and choices. They require much more therapeutic effort to reverse their disorder; many cannot be reversed.

Levels Of Disorders

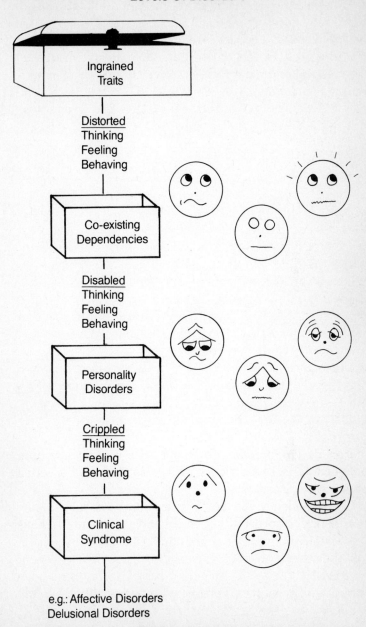

Figure 2.2. Advancing Stages Of Personality Pathology (Millon, modified).

Symptoms Of Co-dependency: Brain Events

Symptoms Group One:
Denial/Delusion (Distorted Thinking)

Delusion occurs when we unconsciously change reality or our reality becomes distorted because we do not use all the information available to us. Usually preceded by denial, either of events or of feelings, it leads to a distortion of our beliefs about the way the world or our family is. We live with our own narrow view of what we see and how we see it. We disavow reality.

Overall this symptom of co-dependency can be characterized as showing distorted thinking on the part of the individual.

In unhealthy families, people are taught either directly or indirectly not to be honest with all they see, hear and feel. They begin to learn in their painful family how to separate themselves from the total view and live with a limited view.

Many of us, in different ways, have dissociated from *how it really was* and chosen to believe *how we want it to be*. When we dissociate from the reality of what we truly feel, we are being dishonest with ourselves.

This leads to distorted thinking, including lying to yourself and to others about the pain you're in. It means that you do not experience the whole picture.

Dissociation

An example of cognitive, affective, behavioral dissociation was given by a patient whose father would come into her bedroom at night from the time that she was about nine years old to the time that she was about 14 and sexually molest her. To this day, she sleeps with her hands in a ball because she said that she learned that when he would come in drunk at night, she would just lie as still yet taut as she could and feel her fingernails digging into her hands. She dissociated by saying, "This is not happening to me," while he sexually molested her.

Her mind (cognitive) said, "This is not happening to me." Her feelings (affective) went numb. Her action (behavioral) was to concentrate on the pain of digging her fingernails into her palms.

**Symptoms Group 1
(Distorted Thinking)**

Preceded By: Denial

Followed By: Dissociation (From Reality)

Figure 3.1. Co-dependency: The Disease

Peter Alsop wrote a song called *Look At The Ceiling*. It's a little girl's story of making up fairy tales about the shadows on the ceiling of her bedroom while her father molests her.

It's much too painful for her to be aware of what is happening, so she creates a fantasy filled with pleasant thoughts. Later on in life she uses the mechanism of dissociation to leave unpleasant situations. This impairs her view of reality.

Dissociation is what happens to the young man whose father said, "Come on, knucklehead, shape up. What kind of a man are you going to grow up to be if you cry?"

From this kind of remark the little boy learns to dissociate from his shame, hurt, guilt and anger. He's living in an environment where he is simply neither rewarded nor acknowledged for feeling feelings.

This little boy also learns to create a "fantasy reality" to escape to whenever he is in emotional pain.

As we begin to dissociate, we become deluded about our reality and lose sight of the truth.

So a big part of delusion is dissociation, the separation of oneself from how it is. All of that adds up to distorted thinking so that, as adults, we're not sure how everything was. Many of us remember the past as being better than it was because we like to have a happy memory.

Symptoms Group Two:
Emotional Repressions
(Distorted Feelings)

Each time we dissociate from reality and deny what is happening, we repress or stuff the feelings that go with the event. Shutting down those feelings leads to a condition of emotional repression. After a while those various feelings that one shuts down become mixed together like a stew. This emotional mixture is called undifferentiated emotion. That means we don't even know what we feel anymore or what the feeling represents. Is it anger, guilt, hurt or shame? What is it? The events also get lost. First of all, we are denying the events and then over time the events and feelings get lost, causing us to experience free-floating feelings such as free-floating anxiety or free-floating anger. It is undifferentiated emotion that churns inside, giving us deep chronic emotional pain.

It is important for us to acknowledge that it is our emotional pain that causes our craving for relief. We crave some kind of relief from what we feel, even though we don't know which feeling we feel.

This craving triggers compulsions (substances and behaviors) which give us temporary relief. A vicious cycle is set in motion. This cycle is described in the chapter on the co-dependency trap.

The first stage of dependency is to seek some sort of change of mood that is pleasurable or rewarding or relief-producing to deal with this craving for relief. Both mood-altering substances and mood-altering behaviors can provide feelings of reward or relief. Different substances and behaviors work for different people.

Some find that one or more of the predictable mood-changing substances, such as alcohol, are effective in producing relief. If a person is set up genetically to react to such mood-changing chemicals, dependency and addiction will begin.

Mood-altering chemicals provide relief from that deeply buried inner pain. It is a temporary relief but for those whose bodies react addictively, it is a potent one which works.

Emotions

Because the healing of our emotional pain is at the core of recovery from co-dependency, we need to digress from the model to share our concept that our emotions are our sixth sense.

Repressed emotions slip out in sarcasm, in arrogance, in irritability, control and isolation. In therapy, we actually have to re-experience the pain in order to release that old emotional abscess.

Example Of An Emotional Abscess

When there is old rage and anger boiling deep inside, it becomes necessary for the person to re-experience that old anger and rage in order to release it. Healing follows release. There are specific therapy models that have been designed to do just that. To heal all feelings, anger, grief, hurt, etc., there needs to be some degree of re-experiencing and release.

That's not to say that we'll never have more painful feelings but the goal of recovery is to feel and acknowledge the feelings, on one hand, and to let go on the other. Some people ask, "If I get rid of all my anger and my hurt and my rage, does that mean that I'll never have to be angry, hurt or rageful again?" The answer is no. All that it means is that with proper help they have the opportunity to re-experience (incise) and get rid of (drain) the emotional abscess that keeps them stuck in today's unhappy life.

Because an emotion is a biochemical action and reaction, emotions have two lives, two senses of energy. When you feel an emotion — which is a message coming from your sensory system — the message says, "React to me, respond to me, do something."

For example, if your sensory system says, "I'm scared," then what you feel is fear and what you might do is run. If your sensory system says to you, "I'm feeling sensual and I'm feeling love and excitement," what you do is express that verbally and nonverbally by responding, by becoming aroused.

Our feelings are a sensory system — something to which we respond.

Our sense of touch is responded to when we pull back from a hot stove or repeatedly stroke a soft piece of velvet or another person.

Our sense of smell is responded to when we leave a place filled with noxious fumes or to purchase fragrances.

Our sense of sight is responded to when we turn or duck — from a flying object or linger over a sunset or piece of art.

Our sense of hearing is responded to when we turn our heads and move our bodies to avoid a blast or we listen to nature or replay a pleasant piece of music.

Our sense of taste is responded to when we spit out bitter or tainted food or when we suck a mint or savor a special sauce.

These five physical senses are interwoven with learning, with memory and with our emotions. Our emotions may be our *sixth sense* and possibly our closest link to reality. They need to be responded to every bit as much as our other five senses.

Receiving Chemical Messages

One can become accustomed to an emotional abscess even while it's growing. Repression becomes so efficient that one's emotions appear to have shrunk or disappeared. It's difficult to ascertain if certain people are happy, sad or excited. They seem to have low energy and no expression. Their feelings are just so piled on top of one another, so intertwined that you can't get any kind of message whatsoever. The feeling that usually rises to the top like cream in milk, however, is anger.

When you get really, really close to someone who has a lot of unexpressed anger, when you get close to their space, you can feel it. You can feel their vibrations.

Have you ever felt that with somebody? What they are doing is giving you chemical messages that are saying, "I'm chuck up to here with old feelings I've never dealt with and my anger is sitting right on my shoulder." The old chip on the shoulder. You can feel vibrations from an angry person; it spills out.

You also can learn to feel welcoming messages. You can learn to read a lot of different kinds of messages, depending on what people have been giving you or not giving you emotionally.

In essence recovery is getting rid of the old abscess of emotional repression, so you can experience your precious feeling life.

How many parents ever said to their kids, "Boy, you got an A in math. That's fantastic. You got an A– in science, terrific! You got an A in expressing your feelings! That's really good!" Not many, if any.

People simply didn't know that our emotional self, our sixth sense, was there to be used. And just as we learn to touch, see, smell, hear and taste and respond to those sensations, we also can learn to feel our emotions and respond to them. A lot of people are walking around emotionally disabled and in pain because they don't know how to do this.

When co-dependents struggle with distorted reality, the second symptom of co-dependency occurs. We repress our feelings. When we do not express what we feel, we repress. Because feelings are a part of each event, the distortion of events and emotions occur simultaneously.

If we don't allow ourselves to cry, to be angry, to grieve and to be vulnerable, then we carry a painful emotional load around composed of all those old angers and irritations. If you never had an opportunity to express your anger and pain when you felt it as a child and during your growing-up years, then you probably still carry that rage today. Many of us have carried a ton of rage with us for a ton of time! We relieve ourselves of the load from time to time by different means, some of which are damaging to ourselves and our relationships with others.

Symptoms Group Three:
Compulsions (Distorted Behavior)

Over the years, for children from painful homes, there has been an inner cesspool or emotional abscess of shame,

**Symptoms Group II
(Distorted Feelings)**

Preceded By Suppression.

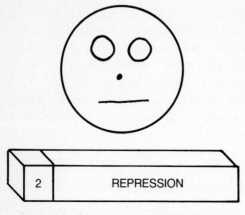

Followed By: Dissociation (From Feelings)

Figure 3.2. Co-dependency: The Disease

hurt, loneliness, anger, inadequacy, sadness and hopeless-
ness. It is deep inside and kept locked away. It hurts and
the need for relief from the pain becomes a craving. Compulsive use of substances and behaviors medicates the
emotional abscess for a while.

The body can become physically dependent on mood-
altering chemicals. This is well known as addiction to
chemicals or chemical dependency. The body also can become physically dependent on certain behaviors. So compulsions to use substances *and/or* behavior become the
armament of the co-dependent.

Crutches Of Compulsion

Mood-altering chemicals provide relief from deeply buried inner pain. It is a temporary relief but for those whose bodies react addictively, it is a potent one which works almost every time. Drugs and alcohol are effective pain-relievers. So is nicotine.

Smoking interferes with the attainment of intimacy and personal growth. Smoking serves as a security blanket — or an insulator from the world of uncertainty and psychic pain.

By turning to cigarettes during times of stress, people are less likely to find strength within themselves. In a sense, for many people, including many recovering drug and alcohol addicts, tobacco is being held onto as that one last crutch.

Smoking interferes with the attainment of intimacy and personal growth. Smoking serves as a security blanket — or an insulator from the world of uncertainty and psychic pain.

Crutches are interesting. When a leg is broken, crutches help you get around. But after the leg has mended, it is vital that the crutch be put back into the closet. Otherwise the leg's muscle will shrivel from disuse and eventually become so weak and withered as to become truly useless — and chronically in need of a crutch.

So many people have withered emotional muscles. For whatever reasons, at some point in our lives we decided to lean upon a drink, some other drug, a cigarette, an unhealthy relationship or something else in order to help deal with emotional discomfort. And it worked for a while. Unfortunately, long after the precipitating events which made smoking or whatever seem so attractive had passed, the crutch remained. And remained and remained. Meanwhile, the emotional muscle deteriorated

beyond its original fragile condition — further increasing
dependence upon the crutch.

There are a variety of crutches and relief-producing
behaviors. Some rushes and some types of relief last 20
minutes, some last 10, some last up to an hour but they all
have one thing in common. As you use them, you begin to
anticipate some kind of "rush" or relief from that anxiety
and pain you feel.

But not everybody is able to get that special kind of relief
from alcohol and drugs. It just doesn't work for everybody
because some people do not have the genetic makeup for it.
There are many people who have painful lives and who
crave relief but alcohol and drugs are not their answer.
They are not any better or any different from drug addicts
or alcoholics, just genetically programmed differently.

Control Crutches

These people find other means, depending on their
circumstances, depending on their family system, depending on what works for them. Some people are set
up to be sugar sensitive and for them sugar does what
alcohol does not.

For families that are very perfectionistic, stoic and cognitive, people are set up to get a rush through the power
of control. In stoic and perfectionistic families, we find
the anorexic, the person who starves and gets a rush
from controlling intake and attention, as well as having a
drive to obtain the "perfect" body. Some get good feelings
from compulsive overeating. Some actually feel a temporary rush and then calmness from purging. Eating disorders are a chronic, progressive and sometimes fatal disease if left untreated.

> *Eating disorders are chronic, progressive and some-
> times fatal diseases if left untreated.*

Anorexia nervosa is a relentless pursuit of thinness which may be characterized by self-starvation, compulsive exercise and laxative abuse. *Bulimia* is the addictive binge/purge cycle characterized by compulsively eating, then purging by self-induced vomiting or laxative and diuretic abuse.

In cognitive, perfectionistic families we also find those addicted to the workaholic rush. These people maintain a certain tolerable level of their internal pain by staying frenetically active and involved.

> *In cognitive, perfectionistic families we also find those addicted to the workaholic rush. These people maintain a certain tolerable level of their internal pain by staying frenetically active.*

They go from one thing to another thing, accomplishing great things . . . or nothing.

People can get a rush in a variety of ways. People can rush with what we call "green-paper" addiction, covering the whole realm of how people spend money. That moves all the way from occasional overspending to living on credit cards, never really believing you have to pay them off. Green-paper addiction includes gambling, which is one of the toughest of the compulsions to treat. The seduction of gambling tends to be a tremendous co-dependency issue.

So drugs, alcohol, nicotine and, for some, sugar and caffeine are major chemical "medicators of emotional pain." They are the most common chemical substances with which we see people form toxic relationships.

Workaholism, eating, purging and not eating, sexual acting out, relationship and sex dependency, controlling and caretaking, as well as spending and gambling, are the most common behavioral "medicators" that co-dependents learn to use for the pain of their emotional abscess.

Intimacy Crutches

Sexuality lends itself very well as an example of a behavioral medicator or compulsion. There are many different ways to look at what happens to people who are struggling with sexual behavioral problems and also sexual dysfunctions. We have learned that sexual acting out as a co-dependency compulsion is treatable.

Some become very dependent on and even skilled in the process and seduction aspects of a relationship. This is because seduction contains a lot of feelings. Seduction is very emotional. You share feelings, you have this stirring inside because of the sharing of information and vulnerability.

For Adult Children or co-dependents who do not have feelings readily available to them, the kind of natural growing seduction that comes out of a natural passion doesn't happen. Instead they may become trapped in a cycle of seduction, only getting their rush from the romantic beginnings of a new sexual relationship or conquest.

But when the excitement of the seduction phase of a relationship ends, they are not able to access their deeper feelings and move on to a genuinely passionate relationship. These people seem to be caught up in a cycle of *love 'em and leave 'em.*

The word *passion* means full of feeling. When we enter into a close relationship, we quickly see that we need the ability to be full of feelings before we can experience intimacy with one another.

Intimacy is the coming together of feelings and may or may not include sexual contact. A term for describing that coming together is *emotional intercourse.*

> *When we enter into a close relationship, we quickly see that we each need the ability to be full of feelings before we can experience intimacy with one another.*

Too many Adult Children and co-dependents have settled for a passionless relationship because their feelings have been medicated by substances or behaviors or both! This is not the same as a sexless relationship.

Symptoms Group III
(Distorted Behavior)

Preceded By Obsession.

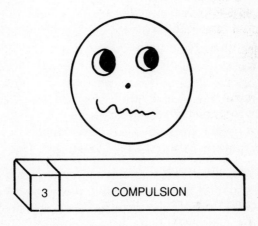

Followed By: Behavioral Dissociation

Figure 3.3. Co-dependency: The Disease

Passion has to do with waking up one's own life and becoming a passionate person. People who have chosen and learned to do that become capable of intimacy and emotional intercourse.

Treatment for the pre-existing emotional abscess and waking up repressed feelings allow a person to act from a passion base and eliminates the need for a sexual behavior medicator in the form of sexual compulsions.

Summary

Whether the compulsive medicator is . . .

- Caretaking
- Refusing food
- Acting out sexually
- Workaholism
- Power/Control
- Nicotine (physical addiction)
- Alcohol (physical addiction)
- Drugs (physical addiction)

The symptom groups of the basic disease of co-dependency are . . .

1. Delusion (distorted thinking).
2. Emotional repression (distorted feeling).
3. Compulsion (distorted behavior).

The word "distorted" indicates a deviation from normal, efficient, full and flexible thinking, feeling and behaving (Stone 1988). Indeed, the disorder of co-dependency appears to be a deviation from normal thinking, feeling and behaving that is an early part of a continuum from mental health to severe mental illness.

Summary Of Brain Events

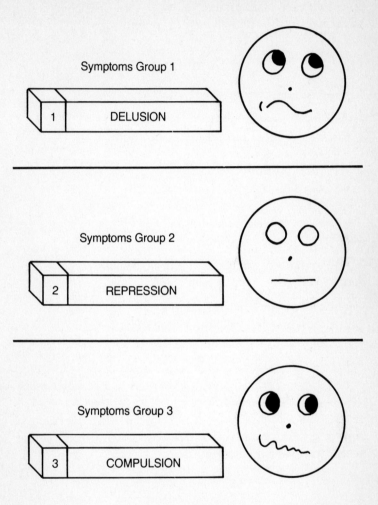

**Figure 3.4. Co-dependency: The Disease.
Summary Of Brain Events**

Complications Of Co-dependency: Life Events

Complications Group One: Low Self-Worth (Disabled Spirituality)

The first complication of co-dependency is chronic low self-worth, which is a condition of feeling shame. There is a difference between guilt and shame.

Guilt is felt when one does something to harm oneself or others.

"I feel badly about something."

The wonderful thing about guilt and the reason guilt can be such a positive feeling is that when I recognize it, I can make amends and then feel good about myself. Guilt has a pattern that brings us back to feeling good if we pursue it. Every bit of guilt can be amended one way or another. So guilt is a very productive feeling. To begin to feel guilty in places where it's appropriate and then to begin to make amends is to be on a straight path to self-worth and healing.

Guilt is the feeling of "I've done something bad and I would like to make amends about it and change."

Guilt is a very productive feeling. To begin to feel guilty in places where it's appropriate and then begin to make amends is to be on a straight path to self-worth and healing.

Complications Group I

Preceded By: Guilt

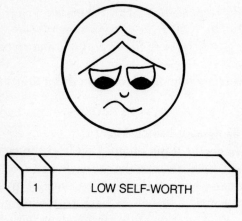

Followed By: Shame

Figure 4.1. Co-dependency: The Problems

Shame is feeling that I am what is bad.

"I am bad, not that I did something bad, I am just faulty. I am bad."

Dysfunctional families tend to produce shame-based people. In hurting families, people bring generations of shame into their current life. What does not get resolved in the generation before comes as a package to the children. It's part of the shame.

Shame can be about:

Alcoholism	*Sexual abuse*
Suicide	*Drug addiction*
Bulimia	*Affairs*
Overweight	*Physical defects*
Anorexia	*Gambling*
Poverty	*Wealth*

It's what came with my package and I feel ashamed about that.

Then when you add in all those old family messages, those inhumane rules, you end up with people who feel less than . . . or unworthy. They end up with chronic low self-worth, which is the state of being based on shame. When we are shame-based, it is difficult to make decisions on what we need for ourselves. People get into perceived powerlessness. They believe they are bad and unworthy and there is nothing they can do to change. Needless to say, this is a self-fulfilling prophecy.

Shame is probably the primary fuel that keeps the disease process of co-dependency running and causes relapses to occur. It is the result, a learned belief or state, rather than the cause of co-dependency. Shame doesn't initiate co-dependency; it results from having the disease of co-dependency. Scratch the paint away from shame, then rage and anger come boiling through. Resolution of that rage and anger refertilizes self-worth and allows the true beauty of the individual to blossom forth.

Low Self-Worth

About every five years there is a current popular new word for low self-worth. It's the kind of self-worth that isn't specific to an event, such as I wish I were as good-looking as Verna; I wish I were as rich as Bill; I wish I were as smart as Marilyn. It's the ongoing constant state of low self-worth that invalidates our right to be. It's the self-worth that says, "I am a faulty person." And it's the self-worth that stays with us so long that we literally grow up believing that we don't even have the right to a full recovery or the right to make choices, changes and decisions for our lives. We relinquish our right to be ourselves.

Many of us were not taught that we are valuable . . . simply because we are. That's all. That's why we are precious . . . We are alive and exist, therefore we are of worth. Many of us believe that our only value is in being valuable to someone else. I am my father's daughter. I am my husband's wife. I am my children's parent. I am my employer's employee and so on. The fact that we are of worth in and of ourselves hardly ever occurs to a low self-worth person.

When low self-worth people do make decisions, they tend to make them lifetime decisions. Low self-worth persons frequently make poor choices personally and professionally. They aren't aware or they can't believe that they can make new choices, that they don't have to stay stuck their entire lives. They become preoccupied with "other"-worth. They get their worth not from self but from others.

The hooks come from others' expectations of us. Hooks need to be removed for us to be free. We need to be detached from our two-way, unhealthy dependencies on our families of origin, our work and even our spouse and children. Detached doesn't mean desertion. Someone might say, "Well, that sounds pretty *self*-centered." This type of self-*centeredness* is actually self-centered or, better yet, "a centered self."

A centered self is a person willing to take such good care of himself that no one else has to. They can set their children free, set their spouse free, set their co-workers free and set themselves free: free to make choices to go, stay, connect, commit, support and love; free to make all of the above choices on a daily basis. This is a position of high self-worth indeed.

Complications Group Two:
Relationship Problems
(Disabled Living)

Our bodies, commanded by our brains, can be put on alert in an instant. That alert is the Alarm Reaction that prepares us to fight or flee.

Dr. Hans Selye wrote extensively on this concept. The Alarm Reaction is the body's ability to instantaneously get ready to stand ground and fight off a saber-toothed tiger, an opponent in a lawsuit or the person on the other side of the tennis net. The opposite of that "fight" alarm is the "flight" alarm, which is the body's ability to instantaneously flee in the interest of self-preservation.

The heart rate and respiratory rate increase. The amount of oxygen going to the muscles is increased. The muscles tense. All senses become hypervigilant.

As we pass through any given day, we use these defense mechanisms many times over. Although we graciously and outwardly restrain our alarm on most occasions, we all have been inwardly at war with our social environment from time to time. That environment consists, in part, of our family life, our social life, our occupational life, our legal life and our financial life.

The co-dependent lives with environmental wars. The smallest unit is the couple. It is rare to find relationship satisfaction when one is emotionally frozen and behaviorally compulsive. Knowing and responding to a partner is simply not the major focus. Beyond the coupling, the family, friends, the job and work environment all suffer from a lack of focus and commitment.

When we are at war with ourself mentally, emotionally and behaviorally, it is very difficult to be in a close, meaningful relationship with someone else. It is no wonder that in recent years, hundreds of books, articles and conferences have focused on "intimacy and relationships." Unfortunately, so many have simplistically suggested that co-dependency is a "relationship" problem, rather than seeing that relationship problems are a *result* and *complication* of co-dependency.

The notion that co-dependency is simply being in a relationship with an alcoholic or an addict is an early observation that occurred in the addictions field. Early in the '70s, it became quite clear that not only were partners and family members affected by being in a relationship with an alcoholic but they were afflicted with their own disabling illness.

Complications Group II

Preceded By: Assumption Of Survival Roles.

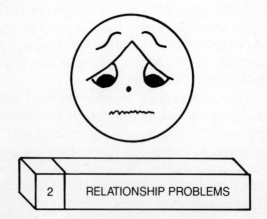

Followed By: Social, Occupational, Legal, Financial, Problems

Figure 4.2. Co-dependency: The Problems

There clearly were problems with . . .

- nicotine addiction
- dependent relationships
- eating disorders
- excessive caretaking
- workaholism . . .

. . . and many more compulsive behaviors. As these behaviors progressed into complications, the families' own illness of co-dependency flourished.

To emphasize only *dependent relationships* and *caretaking* as components of this illness is to understand only a small part of co-dependency. This has been a problem with much of the information in books and literature, which has resulted in mass media confusion.

Learning to face clearly the reality of hurting relationships is the first step of recovery. Next comes the behavioral rebuilding of those relationships one values. Some toxic relationships need to end and others need to be rebuilt. All relationships, whether at work, at home or out in society, deserve attention in co-dependency recovery.

For more satisfying relationships, we recommend two books: *Learning To Love Yourself* will help you to prepare yourself and *Coupleship* will teach you how to build a partnership. Both books are by Sharon Wegscheider-Cruse.

Complications Group Three: Medical Problems (Disabled Physical Functionings)

If because of low self-worth and shame we do not make changes, we will stay stuck. *Stuckness* is another word for a subtle death wish. People who are stuck are beginning the dying process.

Early in this stuckness we start having medical problems. When we do not reach out to ask for what we need and get ourselves nourished, then our bodies go out of harmony, out of alignment, out of ease and they become dis-eased. We make ourselves sick.

When we are functioning in harmony, perceiving ourselves as high functioning, we'll stay healthier. When we
perceive ourselves as low energy, stuck, down, powerless,
we become more susceptible to illness.

The effect of chronic stress on our bodies first produces
many small complaints, ranging from "I'm tired" to "I
ache" and then progresses to organ malfunction, such as
heart irregularity and gastritis to actual organ damage,
such as heart attack or ruptured peptic ulcer.

Stress related disorders are the most common group of
illnesses the physician faces. Our bodies have the ability
to be constantly on guard for danger. "Stress hormones"
such as epinephrine and norepinephrine and cortisone are
released so that our muscle tone, our heart rate, our
breathing rate, our blood pressure, our blood sugar and
other functions are ready to meet a challenge or flee from
danger. Emotional stress, real or imagined, long term or
sudden, calls our stress hormones into play and our body
responds accordingly.

Organ stress can be likened to an engine running at
high RPMs. Every system in our body is going as fast as
it can for as long as it can. Fast regular heartbeats (tachy-
cardia), excess acid in our stomachs (hyperacidity), tense
muscles (myalgia), rapid breathing (tachypnea), increased
adrenalin and insulin secretion (hypoglycemia) are results
of a body put into overdrive.

Then our highly coordinated functions become uncoordinated and we experience malfunctions: irregular heart-
beat, uncoordinated muscles, tremors and shakes, gastritis
and cramps as well as shortness of breath.

Finally actual damage results and the body suffers heart
failure or heart attacks, ruptured ulcers or ulcerative co-
litis. Lung damage, muscle and nerve damage or func-
tional fatigue of our glands also may occur. Ruptured
vessels or blood clots damage our brain, all of which eliminates us from the race.

Similarly it is thought that underwork of our bodies
might accompany depression and pessimism. Low self-
worth can result in a low or nonfunctioning immune sys-

tem. Our immune system helps us ward off infections and cancer. Thus, when the immune system is dampened or suppressed by negative emotions and attitudes, we become susceptible to diseases.

Complications Group III

Preceded By: Organ Stress.

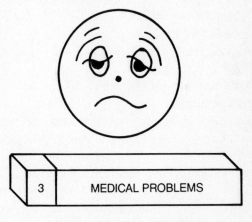

Followed By: Organ Damage

Figure 4.3. Co-dependency: The Problems

Summary

The complications (life events) that arise from having untreated or incompletely treated co-dependency results in complications. This is true for any disease. These complications are remarkably similar to the problems a chemically dependent person encounters. To paraphrase, "When we are powerless over our disease, our life becomes unmanageable."

Summary Of Life Events

Figure 4.4. Co-dependency: The Problems

Treatment And Recovery

The miracle of recovery is there for those who choose to make new choices and decisions.

The good news is that co-dependency is treatable. But what is the best treatment?

Effective Treatment

1. Effective treatment confronts self-delusion with new information. With learning comes understanding and insight and from that comes a reality-based commitment to heal.
2. It creates a safe atmosphere where feelings can surface, to be expressed and discharged so healing can take place. We can't heal what we can't feel.
3. It provides an atmosphere where it is safe and possible to recognize, detox and detach from compulsive medicating behaviors. We can't feel what is medicated.

Recovery needs a program of effective therapy plus a 12-Step support system.

The Co-dependent And Recovery

The co-dependent does best with a two-part recovery program. One part is involvement in a 12-Step group and the other part is a relationship with a co-dependency therapist or a professionally led group.

> *The miracle of recovery is there for those who choose to make new choices and decisions.*

So often we see a co-dependent who is going to three or four different kinds of 12-Step programs and perhaps a leaderless Adult Children of Alcoholics group but is not getting any professional therapy. People in this kind of situation often are confused, angry and overwhelmed. Even though they go to many meetings, they still do not feel focused or in recovery. As people uncover more and more memories and begin to feel more, their life situations become more complex. It is important for these people to get professional care. They need help to make the necessary decisions, to receive guidance while uncovering feelings and to have input and *reality checking* by someone qualified to give it.

> *The major compulsion that one exhibits can be the doorway to a program of recovery. One can work through any compulsion with the 12 Steps and not need to go to separate groups for each issue.*

It is not necessary to go to many different types of 12-Step programs. The focus of 12-Step work is to use the steps to work through solutions rather than rehashing and reliving the problems. These 12-Step groups work well whether one is concerned with compulsive eating, compulsive gambling, compulsive acting-out sexually or any of the other addictions. The major compulsion that one exhibits can be the doorway to a program of recovery. One can work through any compulsion with the 12 Steps and not need to go to separate groups for each issue. One or two groups should suffice, for instance, Alcoholics Anonymous (AA) and Overeaters Anonymous

(OA), Narcotics Anonymous (NA) and Adult Children of Alcoholics (ACoA), etc.

Therefore, we recommend that people pick one or two 12-Step programs to attend that fit with the major compulsion that they are struggling with. They then should reserve time and energy to invest in a therapeutic process that is intense and behavior-change oriented.

When one picks a therapist to work with in co-dependency recovery, it's important to choose someone who thoroughly understands the disease concept of co-dependency. If that person has come from a painful family of his own, it is crucial that he has already received treatment and is healing in his own treatment process.

Therapy can come in many forms. It can be an outpatient program. It can be a short, intense program, lasting from eight to ten days. It is important that the program be designed and facilitated by people who are specifically trained in co-dependency work. Formal continuous therapy can and does come to an end.

> *Formal continuous therapy can and does come to an end.*

Involvement in a 12-Step program can be a much longer commitment. A good treatment program is like emotional surgery: It is a good place to do a lot of work all at once. Emotional surgery is then followed by a period of expert care and is accompanied by long-term healing, which takes place in 12-Step support groups. Prevention of relapse is also provided by 12-Step groups.

Think of recovery as a large beautiful mansion, as in Figure 5.1., with all kinds of doors and rooms for exploration. Here we can find new styles and new horizons. The mansion is there for anyone who wants to walk through a door. One can come in through the door of alcoholism, the door of sexual compulsion, the door of

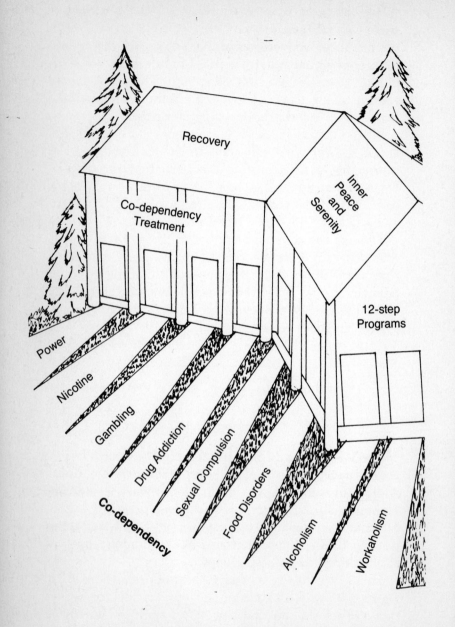

Figure 5.1. Recovery Mansion.

eating disorders or the door of workaholism. Each one of these doors is an entry point that one can recognize for oneself. Once you walk through the door, the differences are diminished and the similarities emphasized.

> *Once you walk through the door, the differences are diminished and the similarities emphasized.*

The disease of co-dependency can be seen as a personal struggle with a variety of compulsive diseases. People walking through the door have lived in a condition of denial, distorted feelings and compulsive behavior, as a result of which they have developed low self-worth, deep shame, inadequacy and anger. All people inside the mansion are exploring and looking for the same recovery route. They are searching for a healing of self. Once through the door, we are all much more alike than different; our differences now can fade and we can focus on recovery in a supportive, simple and clear manner together.

The Disease Results In . . .	Recovery And Healing Require That We . . .
Self-delusion	admit our lives are unmanageable and we need help.
Emotional repression	stop medicating feelings with substances and behaviors and allow ourselves to reconnect with feelings in our life.
Compulsive behavior	become abstinent from toxic substances and moderate compulsive behaviors.
Chronic low self-worth	take the risks and make the changes to care for oneself.

Relationship problems	change behaviors to rebuild valued relationships and end or change toxic ones.
Medical complications	seek appropriate medical help.

Most compulsive behaviors are extreme exaggerations of natural and normal behavior (work, eating, spending, sexuality, etc.) and require moderation for recovery. Use of mood-altering substances, such as drugs or alcohol, requires abstinence for full recovery.

For a complete manual on how to treat co-dependency on an outpatient and/or inpatient basis, see *"Experiential Therapy for Co-dependency"* by the Cruses and George Bougher, Clinical Director, Onsite Training and Consulting, Inc.

Recovering Alcoholics And Addicts

The concept of co-dependency began as a description of the disordered manner in which family members of alcoholics reacted to the drinker, and treatment programs did more to alienate family members than help them create healthy relationships: Chemically dependent versus the co-dependent; the AA member versus the Al-Anon/Alateen member; the "sick (alcoholic) one" versus the "struggling to keep it together ones" (the non-alcoholic family members). The polarity that resulted was great enough in programming and practices that the alcoholic almost became a family **non-member.**

Therapists and counselors reinforced these mistaken attitudes with statements such as:

"Do you agree with the alcoholic or the family members?"

"Should the alcoholics attend this family orientation?"

"I prefer to treat the alcoholic and not the family member."

Such actions, concepts and statements tend to exclude two important factors:

1. The alcoholic/addict *is* a family member.
2. The alcoholic/addict *is* a co-dependent.

Scratch the paint off a chemical dependent and you will find a full-blown co-dependent. Co-dependency accompanies, and usually precedes, chemical dependency. It precipitates but does not cause chemical dependency.

Again, it is important to understand that co-dependency does not cause chemical dependency, other than as a stimulus for the use of certain substance medicators. Genetic programming is probably the major reason that the use of mood-altering drugs provides the degree and type of reinforcement that leads to dependency on chemicals. Ten percent of adults have this programming. An additional ten percent use these chemicals in a medicating and abusive manner.

Symptom Re-emergence

When the substance medicators such as alcohol and nicotine are removed and an individual becomes abstinent, the previously medicated co-dependency symptoms fully emerge once again. (This frequently is seen in psychiatry when, for example, a patient becomes depressed again after a successful anti-depressant is withdrawn.)

Bill W.'s Recovery

Bill Wilson (1895-1971), co-founder of Alcoholics Anonymous and author of the book *12 Steps and 12 Traditions*, suffered greatly from depression and migraines. These even drove him back to certain chemicals in order to gain some degree of relief. He tried megadoses of vitamin E, which caused flushing. He attempted to make a case for its use as an antidepressant for recovering alcoholics. His colleagues discouraged his efforts. He briefly tried LSD and other drugs, being unaware at that time of the problems of cross addiction. Thankfully, he did not relapse into active alcoholism.

The early (1935-1945) and middle (1945-1955) years of AA were tumultuous and chaotic. It took a strong hand and a definite sense of purpose to be the central figure in the movement. Bill's prior alcoholism took its toll on his family, his career and his physical health. He discovered the source of his pathologic compulsions, his controlling of others, his depressions and his migraines, when he discovered his own co-dependency.

His dependency on "people, events and things" outside himself for his self-worth drove him into a *painful sobriety*. Once he realized this and became able to release his dependencies, he became capable of one-way giving. He then became the recipient of the tranquility he had assumed would come with abstinence. He finally attained *emotional sobriety* as well. He began his recovery from the disorder of co-dependency without even knowing its name. Here is his story . . .

> *There is no need to suffer through a painful sobriety.*

Love

The Next Frontier
Emotional Sobriety
by Bill W.

I think that many oldsters who have put our AA "booze cure" to severe but successful tests still find they often lack emotional sobriety. Perhaps they will be the spearhead for the next major development in AA — the development of much more real maturity and balance (which is to say, humility) in our relations with ourselves, with our fellows and with God.

Those adolescent urges that so many of us have for top approval, perfect security and perfect romance — urges quite appropriate to age 17 — prove to be an impossible way of life when we are at age 47 or 57.

Since AA began, I've taken immense wallops in all these areas because of my failure to grow up, emotionally and spiritually. My God, how painful it is to keep demanding the impossible and how very painful to discover finally that all along we have had the cart before the horse! Then comes the final agony of seeing how awfully wrong we have been, but still finding ourselves unable to get off the emotional merry-go-round.

How to translate a right mental conviction into a right emotional result and so into easy, happy and good living — well, that's not only the neurotic's problem, it's the problem of life itself for all of us who have got to the point of real willingness to hew to right principles in all our affairs.

Even then, as we hew away, peace and joy will still elude us. That's the place so many of us AA oldsters have come to. And it's a hell of a spot, literally. How shall our unconscious — from which so many of our fears, compulsions and phony aspirations still stream — be brought into line with what we actually believe, know and want? How to convince our dumb, raging and hidden "Mr. Hyde" becomes our main task.

I've recently come to believe that this can be achieved. I believe so because I begin to see many benighted ones — folks like you and me — commencing to get results. Last autumn [several years back — ed.] depression, having no really rational cause at all, almost took me to the cleaners. I began to get scared that I was in for another long chronic spell. Considering the grief I've had with depressions, it wasn't a bright prospect.

I kept asking myself, "Why can't the 12 Steps work to release depression?" By the hour, I stared at the St. Francis Prayer . . . "It's better to comfort than to be comforted." Here was the formula all right. But why didn't it work?

Suddenly I realized what the matter was. My basic flaw had always been dependence — almost absolute dependence — on people or circumstances to supply me with prestige, security and the like. Failing to get these things according to my perfectionist dreams and specifications, I had fought for them. And when defeat came, so did my depression.

There wasn't a chance of making the outgoing love of St. Francis a workable and joyous way of life until these fatal and almost absolute dependencies were cut away.

Because I had over the years undergone a little spiritual development, the absolute quality of these frightful dependencies had never before been so starkly revealed. Reinforced by what Grace I could secure in prayer, I found I had to exert every ounce of will and action to cut off these faulty emotional dependencies upon people, upon AA, indeed, upon any set of circumstances whatsoever.

Then only could I be free to love as St. Francis had. Emotional and instinctual satisfactions, I saw, were really the extra dividends of having love, offering love and expressing a love appropriate to each relationship of life.

Plainly, I could not avail myself of God's love until I was able to offer it back to Him by loving others as He would have me. And I couldn't possibly do that so long as I was victimized by false dependencies.

For my dependency meant demand — a demand for the possession and control of the people and the conditions surrounding me.

While those words "absolute dependency" may look like a gimmick, they were the ones that helped to trigger my release into my present degree of stability and quietness of mind, qualities which I am now trying to consolidate by offering love to others regardless of the return to me.

This seems to be the primary healing circuit: an outgoing love of God's creation and His people, by means of which we avail ourselves of His love for us. It is most clear that the real current can't flow until our paralyzing dependencies are broken and broken at depth. Only then can we possibly have a glimmer of what adult love really is.

Spiritual calculus, you say? Not a bit of it. Watch any AA of six months working with a new Twelfth Step case. If the case says, "To the devil with you," the Twelfth Stepper only smiles and turns to another case. He doesn't feel frustrated or rejected. If his next case responds and in turn starts to give love and attention to other alcoholics, yet gives none back to him, the sponsor is happy about it anyway. He still doesn't feel rejected; instead he rejoices that his one-time prospect is sober and happy. And if his next case turns out in later time to be his best friend (or romance), then the sponsor is most joyful. But he well knows that his happiness is a by-product — the extra dividend of giving without any demand for a return.

The really stabilizing thing for him was having and offering love to that strange drunk on his doorstep. That was St. Francis at work, powerful and practical, minus dependency and minus demand.

In the first six months of my own sobriety, I worked hard with many alcoholics. Not a one responded. Yet this work kept me sober. It wasn't a question of those alcoholics giving me anything. My stability came out of trying to give, not out of demanding that I receive.

Thus I think it can work out with emotional sobriety. If we examine every disturbance we have, great or small, we will find at the root of it some unhealthy dependency and its consequent unhealthy demand. Let us, with God's help, continually surrender these hobbling demands. Then we can be set free to live and love; we may then be able to Twelfth Step ourselves and others into emotional sobriety.

Of course, I haven't offered you a really new idea — only a gimmick that has started to unhook several of my own "hexes" at depth. Nowadays my brain no longer races compulsively in either elation, grandiosity or depression. I have been given a quiet place in bright sunshine.

Self-Assessment

How do you know if you are suffering from co-dependency (co-existing dependencies)?

We have described the signs, symptoms and complications of the disease. The following groups of self-assessment characteristics deal with each group of symptoms and complications.

Characteristics Of Denial

□ 1. Do you avoid reflecting on unpleasant thoughts?

□ 2. Are you a Pollyanna about difficulties?

□ 3. Do you withdraw into reveries to fulfill needs?

□ 4. Do you exhibit magical thinking or superstitious beliefs?

□ 5. Are you minimally introspective with a barren inner world?

□ 6. Do you fabricate events to bolster self-illusions?

□ 7. If you are not introspective, do you internalize experiences poorly?

□ 8. Do you minimize?

□ 9. Do you see things as they are or the way you wished they were?

□ 10. Are you irritated by others' assessment of you or the manner in which you behave?

□ 11. Are you frequently very confused by what's happening in your life?

Characteristics Of Repression

☐   1. Do you have trouble showing your feelings?

☐   2. Are you phlegmatic and lacking in spontaneity?

☐   3. Do you procrastinate and put things off?

☐   4. Do you appear lethargic and lacking in vitality?

☐   5. Are you emotionally impassive or unaffectionate?

☐   6. Are you cold and humorless but edgy?

☐   7. Do you have mood shifts from dejection to anger to apathy?

☐   8. Are you unable to experience pleasure in depth?

☐   9. Do you restrain warmth and affection?

☐ 10. Do you vacillate between being anguished and numb?

☐ 11. Do you try to keep emotions under tight control?

Characteristics Of Compulsion

☐   1. Do you seem attracted to risk, danger and harm?

☐   2. Do you maintain a regulated and highly organized lifestyle?

☐   3. Are you excessively devoted to work/productivity?

☐   4. Do you suffer from eating disorders?

☐   5. Do you suffer from nicotine addiction?

☐   6. Do you suffer from sexual preoccupation and/or acting out?

☐   7. Do you suffer from exercise excess?

☐   8. Do you suffer from gambling and/or spending problems?

☐   9. Are you an excessive caretaker?

☐ 10. Are you highly self-disciplined?

☐ 11. Do you have chronic feelings of emptiness or boredom?

☐ 12. Do you actively seek attention and solicit praise?

☐ 13. Are you competitive and power-oriented?

☐ 14. Do you sustain monogamous relationships?

☐ 15. Do you insist others do things your way?

☐ 16. Do you constantly seek recognition and admiration?

Characteristics Of Low Self-Worth

☐ 1. Do you volunteer to do unpleasant tasks to gain approval?

☐ 2. Do you anxiously anticipate ridicule/humiliation?

☐ 3. Have you made suicidal threats or attempts?

☐ 4. Do you undermine your own good fortunes?

☐ 5. Do you place yourself in inferior or demeaning positions?

☐ 6. Do you act arrogantly self-assured and super confident?

☐ 7. Do you fail to complete tasks beneficial to yourself?

☐ 8. Do you feel dejected or guilty after positive experiences?

☐ 9. Are you compliant, submissive and placating?

☐ 10. Are you uninterested in people who treat you well?

☐ 11. Do you appear indifferent to praise or criticism?

☐ 12. Do you engage in self-sacrifice and martyrdom?

☐ 13. Do you feel helpless or uncomfortable when alone?

☐ 14. Do you chase after people who treat you poorly?

Characteristics Of Relationship Problems

☐   1. Do you seem socially aloof and remote?

☐   2. Do you have difficulty doing things on your own?

☐   3. Do you tend to socially isolate?

☐   4. Do you control interpersonal relationships?

☐   5. Are you relationship dependent?

☐   6. Do you go to great lengths to avoid being alone?

☐   7. Do you provoke rejection, then feel hurt or humiliated?

☐   8. Are you devastated when close relationships end?

☐   9. Are you fearful of loss or desertion?

☐ 10. Are you drawn to relationships in which you will suffer?

☐ 11. Do you have close friends or intimates?

☐ 12. Do you stay in problem relationships fearing abandonment?

☐ 13. Do you have a pattern of unstable and intense relationships?

Characteristics Of Organ Dysfunction

☐   1. Do you show little desire for sexual experience?

☐   2. Do you frequently worry about your heart, blood pressure or having cancer?

☐   3. Are you preoccupied about the shape or appearance of your body?

☐   4. Do you visit a physician frequently for different problems?

☐   5. Do you have high blood pressure or heart irregularities?

☐   6. Do you have numerous stomach, bowel and bladder problems?

☐   7. Do you have numerous headaches, insomnia or backaches?

☐   8. Have you had actual organ damage — heart at-
        tack, ulcers or arthritis?

If you find that many of these characteristics apply to
you and are uncomfortable or painful in your life but
not disabling, then it might serve you well to apply *Plan
1 For Recovery*.

However, if you find your characteristics are becoming
increasingly painful and more disabling, then you might
want to move to *Plan 2 For Recovery*.

These two plans are given on the following page.

Plans For Recovery

Plan 1

1. Join one or two different 12-Step support groups to address the more disabling primary compulsions. Fit all other compulsions into these two meetings. Find groups that concentrate on solutions, not problems.

Plan 2

2. Seek treatment with someone specifically trained in co-dependency treatment. Treat your recovery as you would any other medical recovery: intensive care, aftercare and a change to a healthy lifestyle. You might choose an outpatient therapist, an outpatient program or an intensive residential program.

How To Choose A Therapist Or Treatment Program

It is important to interview a potential therapist or program. Some suggested questions are . . .

1. Have you and/or your staff received specific training in treating co-dependency?
2. Are you and/or your staff free of nicotine, alcohol and drug abuse?
3. Are you and/or your staff supportive of 12-Step self-help groups?
4. Are you and/or your staff trained in experiential therapy (Gestalt, psychodrama, etc.)?

READER/CUSTOMER CARE SURVEY

We care about your opinions! Please take a moment to fill out our online Reader Survey at **http://survey.hcibooks.com**.

As a **"THANK YOU"** you will receive a **VALUABLE INSTANT COUPON** towards future book purchases as well as a **SPECIAL GIFT** available only online! Or, you may mail this card back to us and we will send you a copy of our exciting catalog with your valuable coupon inside.

(PLEASE PRINT IN ALL CAPS)

First Name _____ MI. _____ Last Name _____

Address _____ City _____

State _____ Zip _____ Email _____

1. Gender
- ☐ Female ☐ Male

2. Age
- ☐ 8 or younger
- ☐ 9-12 ☐ 13-16
- ☐ 17-20 ☐ 21-30
- ☐ 31+

3. Did you receive this book as a gift?
- ☐ Yes ☐ No

4. Annual Household Income
- ☐ under $25,000
- ☐ $25,000 - $34,999
- ☐ $35,000 - $49,999
- ☐ $50,000 - $74,999
- ☐ over $75,000

5. What are the ages of the children living in your house?
- ☐ 0 - 14 ☐ 15+

6. Marital Status
- ☐ Single
- ☐ Married
- ☐ Divorced
- ☐ Widowed

7. How did you find out about the book?
(please choose one)
- ☐ Recommendation
- ☐ Store Display
- ☐ Online
- ☐ Catalog/Mailing
- ☐ Interview/Review

8. Where do you usually buy books?
(please choose one)
- ☐ Bookstore
- ☐ Online
- ☐ Book Club/Mail Order
- ☐ Price Club (Sam's Club, Costco's, etc.)
- ☐ Retail Store (Target, Wal-Mart, etc.)

9. What subject do you enjoy reading about the most?
(please choose one)
- ☐ Parenting/Family
- ☐ Relationships
- ☐ Recovery/Addictions
- ☐ Health/Nutrition
- ☐ Christianity
- ☐ Spirituality/Inspiration
- ☐ Business Self-help
- ☐ Women's Issues
- ☐ Sports

10. What attracts you most to a book?
(please choose one)
- ☐ Title
- ☐ Cover Design
- ☐ Author
- ☐ Content

TAPE IN MIDDLE; DO NOT STAPLE

BUSINESS REPLY MAIL
FIRST-CLASS MAIL PERMIT NO 45 DEERFIELD BEACH, FL

POSTAGE WILL BE PAID BY ADDRESSEE

Health Communications, Inc.
3201 SW 15th Street
Deerfield Beach FL 33442-9875

FOLD HERE

Comments

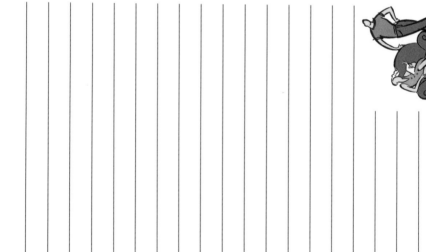

Study
Group
Guidelines

Group Study Guides For
Understanding Co-dependency

Co-dependency recovery is possible and recovery rates run high. One of the best tools for finding a fully ongoing recovery is the daily use of the 12 Steps of recovery of Alcoholics Anonymous and Al-Anon as guides for living problems. Additionally the use of professional and self-help groups is one of the best tools for aiding ourselves in overcoming our distorted thinking.

Twelve-Step study groups have found it useful to examine each aspect of their disorder and recovery process. Using group insight and sharing exceeds the benefits of individual study. As recovery proceeds new perspectives and increased insight and emotional sharing results from *repeating* the study sessions. Emotional pain diminishes as self-worth and gratitude increase.

The following ten suggested study sessions will help a group to stimulate risk-taking and sharing. Understanding, self-awareness, hope and relief of emotional pain begin to take place.

The ten suggested study sessions are each coordinated with certain sections of the book and are broken into . . .

- Introduction/Self-Assessment
- Explanation
- Discussion
- Into Action.

As in book study groups or Step study groups, group reading sets the tone and invites participation by members. A leader of the group might begin with the Introduction/Self-Assessment and then invite group member(s) to share reading parts of the Explanation. This is then followed by spontaneous Discussion after which the group leader can share the Into Action statement as a summary of the study session.

Study Session 1 — The Trap

Introduction/Self-Assessment

Do I feel that I live my life going in circles, repeating the same mistakes, stuck in situations I don't want to be in but afraid to change? Do I *hurt* a lot, perhaps not even knowing why? Does gratitude, feeling good about myself and excitement with living only come to me in spurts followed by more hurts?

Explanation

Read together Section 1 page 14 to page 20, The Co-dependency Trap.

Discussion

Suggestion — Group members share examples of substance and/or behavioral medicators that have increased in frequency of use, duration, intensity and variety.

Into Action

"Now is the time to realize that I'm tired of the way it is and begin a diligent search to understand the trap of present disorder and what I can do about it! I have work to do!"

Study Session 2 — Denial

Introduction/Self-Assessment

How does denial work? What is it? Do I do it? Are many of my attitudes, opinions and behaviors a form of denying reality, the way it really is?

Read together Section 7, Characteristics Of Denial, page 81.

Explanation

Read together, Section 3, Symptoms Group One: Denial/Delusion (Distorted Thinking), pages 33 to 35.

Discussion

Suggestion — Participants share recent examples of their denial and minimizing.

Into Action

"Now is the time to accept reality by keeping an open mind and listening to the opinions of others regarding my denial and minimizing. Now is the time for total self-honesty!"

Study Session 3 — Emotional Repression

Introduction/Self-Assessment

What feelings am I avoiding and keeping inside? Am I honest with myself and others about my angers, my hurts, my fears, my loneliness, etc.? Do I really know

what feelings are and what their purpose is? Can I actually recognize a feeling?

Read together Section 7, Characteristics Of Repression,
page 82.

Explanation

Read together Section 3, Symptoms Group Two, Emotional Repressions (Distorted Feelings), pages 35 to 36.

Discussion

Suggestion — Participants share rules regarding emotions in their family of origin and how those rules still
have power.

Into Action

"Now is the time to let myself feel my feelings in a
safe manner and in a safe place. Being in a group may be
one of the first places to begin recapturing and using my
feeling life."

Study Session 4 —
Compulsive Behavior

Introduction/Self-Assessment

What compulsive behaviors do I use to keep my feelings
medicated, to give me a temporary high or to minimize the
low? What substances (e.g., alcohol, drugs, nicotine, etc.)
do I use or what people, institutions or occupations do I
use to make me feel worthwhile? Do self-defeating compulsive, repetitive behaviors (e.g., workaholism, control
and caretaking, eating, not eating, purging, sexual acting
out, shopping, gambling, excess exercise) keep me busy,
distracted and unable to make new choices and changes?

Read together Section 7, Characteristics Of Compulsion, pages 82 to 83.

Explanation

Read together Section 3, Symptoms Group Three, Compulsions (Distorted Behavior), pages 39 to 42.

Discussion

Suggestion — Participants share their "Big Three" compulsions that they have been dependent upon at one time or another. Identify them as *co-existing dependencies* (co-dependency) whether they are dependencies on substances or behaviors or a combination of both.

Into Action

"Now is the time to stop medicating myself with repetitive self-defeating behaviors. I cannot heal what I cannot feel and I cannot feel what I medicate. If I can stop these behaviors, I will. If I cannot stop these behaviors, or I trade them for more destructive and disabling ones, I will seek professional care to help me."

Study Session 5 — Low Self-Worth

Introduction/Self-Assessment

Do I struggle with my self-worth? Is it difficult to make choices and act on my own behalf? Many of us have been reprimanded for being self-centered and conceited without explaining the difference between this and a high level of self-worth and self-confidence. We are taught and learn on our own to deprecate ourselves . . . many times to the degree that when some bad event befalls us, we say, "I probably deserved that . . . "

Read together Section 7, Characteristics Of Low Self-Worth, pages 83.

Explanation

Read together Section 4, Complications Group One, Low Self-Worth (Disabled Spirituality), pages 51 to 54.

Discussion

Suggestion — Participants share their perceptions of self at different ages or participants discuss current experiences between humility and humiliation; between self-worth and vanity.

Into Action

"Now is the time for me to accept myself, especially my inner childlike self, as a worthy person. As I share more about myself and find myself acceptable to those around me, I can accept myself more fully and believe in my own worth."

Study Session 6 — Relationships

Introduction/Self-Assessment

Have I become too dependent on others, especially certain others (lover, friends, boss, heroes, professionals), so that I now feel and appear unsafe and needy? Or the opposite . . . have I begun to isolate and resist intimacy? In either case I am spending a great amount of time preoccupied with and controlling others. Either way, dependent or isolated, it is probably the result of not having a good relationship with myself. A healthy relationship requires a healthy self.

Read together Section 7, Characteristics Of Relationship Problems, page 84.

Explanation

Read together Section 4, Complications Group Two, Relationship Problems (Disabled Living), pages 55 to 57.

Discussion

Suggestion — Participants share their use of control, enmeshment, dependency, isolation and aloofness in their relationships. The key words are . . .

- Intimacy
- Passion
- Fight and flight
- Independence.

Into Action

"Now is the time for me to grow in knowledge about myself. It is important for me to think for myself, to feel and share my feelings, even when risky. As I learn to maintain myself, I can better maintain my emotional investments into friendships and relationships. As I learn to better maintain relationships, I am then best prepared for a meaningful and healthful primary relationship . . .

Study Session 7 — Medical Problems

Introduction/Self-Assessment

Has my co-dependency affected my health? Has or does my body suffer from stress-related disorders? Am I so caught up in surviving, watching, scrambling and worrying that I fail to maintain good health habits, follow healthy eating, sleeping and exercise patterns? Am I ignoring signals my body may be sending me? Signals that might be saying "slow down" or "check this out" or "something needs fixing"?

Read together Section 7, Characteristics Of Organ Dysfunction, page 84.

Explanation

Read together, Section 4, Complications Group Three: Medical Problems (Disabled Physical Functionings), pages 57 to 59.

Discussion

Suggestion — Participants share any preoccupations with body image, sleep patterns, energy patterns, last visit to physician/dentist and past histories of stress-related disorders. Share physical recovery stories.

Into Action

"Now is the time to take good care of myself in every way, including physically. I will pay attention to what I eat, I will commit to regular exercise and regular medical and dental care as a part of my recovery program."

Study Session 8 — Choices And Risks

Introduction/Self-Assessment

Have my compulsions robbed me of the power of choice? Am I so busy doing that I am unable to hold still and just be? Is my fear of loss and abandonment so great that I am powerless to make the very choices and changes that would eliminate my compulsions and fears? Recovery demands choices and changes. Choices and changes demand risk-taking without a guarantee. Can I make a choice without a guarantee that it's the right choice? Do I have the faith that I can make a choice and *make* it the right choice? And if it seems not to be the right choice, to learn from that and move on to further choicemaking?

Re-read together Section 7, Characteristics Of Compulsion, page 82.

Explanation

Read together the following excerpt from *Choicemaking* by Sharon Wegscheider-Cruse.

> Does the Ideal Choicemaker go his/her own way alone, aloof, carefree and independent? Not at all. Choicemakers stay concerned and interested in others, but Choicemakers do not allow that concern and care to become the center of their existence. As Choicemakers we will direct our own lives as much as possible, without seeking control over others and without letting ourselves be subservient to another's opinions or feelings.
>
> We will learn to decide if we want to have a career or stay at home. A choice, *not* an expectation.
>
> We will decide whether to adhere to family traditions or start some of our own.
>
> We will choose whether to have a career change or stay with an early-chosen profession.
>
> We will learn to take care of ourselves and negotiate our involvement in relationships.
>
> As Choicemakers we won't necessarily always like what we see each other do or what we hear each other say. But we'll feel free to share with fellow Choicemakers what we don't like for the sole purpose of sharing or enhancing understanding. We are not to remold others in our image. In respect for each other's personhood, we will let each other decide whether to change or not. Anything less in this sharing process is covered-up manipulation.
>
> Once we succeed in taking the first steps toward our own freedom in personal responsibility, we can choose to share our "self" with someone else in a relationship of our *choice*. We won't just *fall* in love with someone, we won't be mindlessly swept away. We will find someone we can choose to love.
>
> As Choicemakers, we will cultivate friendships that are

mutally rewarding, mutually enriching. We will learn the value of choosing to move away from relationships that bring us down, that thwart our self-worth. We will learn to abandon, if necessary, lifestyles encumbered with negative thoughts and feelings. As Choicemakers, we take the initiative to surround ourselves with individuals who bring out the very best in us and help us on our inner journey toward goodness, love and inner peace . . .

Our imperfections have a symptom — pain. And pain signals dysfunction, injury or some dis-ease that requires something to change before relief can occur. That something is frequently us. One of the more unexpected side-effects of change turns out to be growth.

But there are times when that pain is like a rock in our shoe — almost imperceptible, bearable and unimportant, as compared to the immediate task at hand. Then after we remove it, its actual importance becomes clear. Now we see the deep impression it has made, and almost immediately we feel the relief and freedom and regained agility when we remove the rock. We look at our wounds and blisters in disbelief that we could have denied their seriousness, or even their presence, and certainly their influence for so long.

But no matter the number of stones that find their way into our shoes, the human spirit, once enlightened, continues to look up and hope and learn and delight in each lesson. The human spirit continues to choose and change — and continues to remove stones one by one.

Choicemaking

Every day I have before me many choices,
It is not easy to choose,
For often the choice means letting go
>*of the past*
>*of the present*

I know what the past was.
I know what the present is.
But choice propels me into the future.
I'm not sure I'll make the right choices.

It's not easy to "let go."
It's not easy to fly into the future.
It's like the space between trapezes.
It's not knowing whether you're going to be caught.
It's not knowing whether you're going to fall.

It's not easy to live in trust.
That space between trapezes requires faith.
I must admit that my faith is often shaky.
I pray and hope that I'll make good decisions,
That I'll be caught and will not fall.

Every day I have before me many choices.

To become healthy, to become whole means that one must take responsibility for oneself. One must become a Choicemaker every step of the way. For a co-dependent who has spent years watching, weighing alternatives, afraid to make a mistake . . . often passively waiting for others to decide . . . becoming a Choicemaker can be a formidable task.

Yet Choicemaking is the foundation that recovery builds on. Choicemaking makes recovery possible.

Discussion

Suggestion — Participants share their most difficult recent choice and a possible future choice. Also how does choicemaking change as recovery continues.

Into Action

"Now is the time to want to change. If I haven't liked the way my life is going, then I must make changes in it and me. Changes are dependent on choices and choices are needed now."

Study Session 9 — Forgiveness And Amends

Introduction/Self-Assessment

Full recovery means letting go of old bitterness and resentments. The emotions of bitterness drain our energy and cloud our thinking. Those for whom we hold resentment live in our heads *Rent Free*. Have I forgiven those who have wronged me? Am I preoccupied with past injuries done to me, even those of long ago? And do I still carry pain, shame and guilt for the wrongs I have done to others?

Explanation

Many times we have apologized and many times others have apologized to us. The need for the ongoing use of our ability to forgive and to be forgiven is extremely important in our recovery. Many times we fail to remember that we have the capacity and ability and even the need to forgive others and to accept their request for us to forgive them. Forgiveness is almost always a two-way street. If you cannot make amends, you suffer. If you cannot accept amends from others, you also suffer. If you cannot accept an apology, then you cannot forgive. An apology is a request for your forgiveness.

If you cannot request another person's forgiveness, then it is likely you are not ready to forgive them if they refuse your request. It sounds complicated and as if it is going in a circle, but it really isn't circular.

It is like a tennis match. It only takes one to serve and that's all a person can do. If a serve is returned, then there is a match. Both individuals benefit. But if no one receives your serve, there is no match. If you have made an apology to someone and have asked for their forgiveness and they have failed to do so, then no further action is necessary on your part. No two-way negotiation will take place. Even so, you can receive relief from your fear and anger and resentment toward them and the events that caused you discomfort in the first place.

Such relief often comes by simply asking for their forgiveness. Whether or not you receive it, it pays to practice your serve.

One exercise that we have found helpful is to make a list of . . .

1. Some people who have hurt you in your life need to ask for *your* forgiveness. If they do, can you forgive them?
2. Some people whom you have hurt need you to ask for their forgiveness. Can you do it?

3. Some words that describe how you feel or what you do when you have been hurt.
4. Some people whom you have seen suffer from their inability to forgive. List the number of years it's been since the event occurred that they have been unable to forgive.

The exercise part of this is if you are unable to do number 1 or perform number 2, you will probably also feel number 3 for the number of years you listed in number 4.

Into Action

"Now is the time for me to give a realistic look at how much of my emotional energy is spent unnecessarily over old resentments and the guilt I carry for not having made proper amends. Now is the time to understand that I can heal through making the proper amends and being prepared to receive amends from others. I must now identify my needs and desires, which will require that I identify all the losses, both real and unreal. For those real losses I must grieve the loss and feel the pain. To avoid the pain is to avoid an emotion, to avoid reality and, therefore, start chasing a myth. I realize that forgiveness can only come about in reality. This is the time to make a list of all those I have harmed and be willing to make amends to them whenever possible, except when to do so would injure them or others." (As suggested in the 12 Steps.)

**Study Session 10 —
Recovery And Living**

Introduction/Self-Assessment

The happiness we all seek from recovery can sometimes escape us if we overdo the process. Our search for the very best path or exactly the right answers results in a constant searching pattern, which causes us to pass up good methods of recovery that would work perfectly well if we would just stop and let them. Until we stop chasing after solutions or stop working *on* problems rather than *through* problems, we cannot help anyone else in their recovery. We cannot give away or share that which we do not have. Am I still on a frantic search? Do I still shrug off opportunities to recover because they don't seem just right for me? Am I a good example to others of how to live life? Am I ready to enjoy the benefits of truly giving to others, of doing someone a favor without being found out?

Explanation

Read together Section 5, Treatment and Recovery, pages 65 to 70. Also, portions of Section 6, Love by Bill W., pages 75 to 78.

Into Action

"Now is the time for me to set limits on the acute process of recovery. I will always have a program of living but I do not want a lifetime or lifestyle of therapy. My life will become centered and balanced so I will be able to become a full-fledged participant in life with those I choose, in the places I choose and at the times I choose. Then I will have much to offer and will experience the joy of helping each time I *pass it on*."

BIBLIOGRAPHY

Ackerman, Robert J. **Perfect Daughters: Adult Daughters Of Alcoholics.** Deerfield Beach, FL: Health Communications, 1989.

Ackerman, Robert J. and Pickering, Susan E. **Abused No More: Recovery For Women From Abusive Or Co-dependent Relationships.** Blue Ridge Summit, PA: Tab Books, Inc. 1989.

Ashton, Heather. **Brain Systems Disorders And Psychotropic Drugs.** Oxford, UK: OUP, 1987.

Bozarth, Michael. **In Brain Reward Systems And Abuse.** New York: Raven Press, 1987.

Cermak, Timmen L., **A Time To Heal: The Road To Recovery For Adult Children Of Alcoholics.** New York: Avon Books, 1988.

Cloninger, C. Robert. **A Systematic Method For Clinical Description And Classification Of Personality Variants.** *Archives of General Psychiatry* (June 1987).

Coyle, Joseph T. "Neuroscience And Psychiatry." In **Textbook Of Psychiatry.** Washington, DC: American Psychiatric Press, 1988.

Cruse, Joseph R. **Painful Affairs: Looking For Love Through Addiction And Co-dependency.** Deerfield Beach, FL: Health Communications, 1989.

Diagnostic and Statistical Manual III-R. Washington, DC: American Psychiatric Association, 1987.

Fibiger, H.C., and Phillips, A.G. **In Brain Reward Systems And Abuse.** New York: Raven Press, 1987.

Gorski, Terence T. "Defining Co-dependence." Paper presented at National Forum on Co-dependence, Scottsdale, AZ, Sept. 1989.

Millon, Theodore, and Everly, George S., Jr. **Personality And Its Disorders: A Biosocial Learning Approach.** New York: Wiley, 1985.

Millon, Theodore. **Millon Clinical Multiaxial Inventory-II: Manual For The MCMI-II.** Second Edition. Minneapolis, MN: National Computer Systems, Inc., 1987.

————. "Personalogic Psychotherapy: Ten Commandments For A Posteclectic Approach To Integrative Treatment." Paper presented at the Annual Meeting of the Society for the Exploration of Psychotherapy Integration, Evanston, IL, May 1987.

Restak, Richard M. **The Mind.** New York: Bantam, 1988.

Stone, Evelyn M. **American Psychiatric Glossary.** Washington, DC: American Psychiatric Press, Inc., 1988.

Washton, Arnold, and Boundy, Donna. **Willpower's Not Enough: Understanding And Recovering From Addiction Of Every Kind.** New York: Harper & Row, 1989.

Wegscheider, Sharon. **The Family Trap.** Rapid City, SD: Nurturing Networks, 1976.

————. **Another Chance: Hope And Healing For The Alcoholic Family.** Palo Alto, CA: Science and Behavior Books, 1981.

————. **Learning To Love Yourself.** Pompano Beach, FL: Health Communications, 1987.

————. **Coupleship.** Deerfield Beach, FL: Health Communications, 1988.

Books from . . .
Health Communications

PERFECT DAUGHTERS: *Adult Daughters Of Alcoholics*
Robert Ackerman
Through a combined narrative of professional and anecdotal styles Robert Ackerman helps restore a sense of balance in life for Adult Daughters of Alcoholics.
ISBN 1-55874-040-6 $8.95

I DON'T WANT TO BE ALONE:
For Men And Women Who Want To Heal Addictive Relationships
John Lee
John Lee describes the problems of co-dependent relationships and his realization that he may be staying in such a relationship because of his fear of being alone.
ISBN 1-55874-065-1 $8.95

SHAME AND GUILT: Masters Of Disguise
Jane Middelton-Moz
The author uses myths and fairy tales to portray different shaming environments and to show how shame can keep you from being the person you were born to be.
ISBN 1-55874-072-4 $8.95

LIFESKILLS FOR ADULT CHILDREN
Janet G. Woititz and Alan Garner
This book teaches you the interpersonal skills that can make your life easier while improving your sense of self-worth. Examples are provided to help clarify the lessons and exercises are given for practicing your new skills.
ISBN 1-55874-070-8 $8.95

THE MIRACLE OF RECOVERY:
Healing For Addicts, Adult Children And Co-dependents
Sharon Wegscheider-Cruse
This is about the good news — that recovery from co-dependency is possible. Sharon offers ways to embrace the positive aspects of one's experience — to realize the strength that can come from adversity. Celebrate your own miracle with this inspiring book.
ISBN 1-55874-024-4 $9.95

3201 S.W. 15th Street,
Deerfield Beach, FL 33442-8124
1-800-851-9100

Health Communications, Inc.

Other Books By . . .
Health Communications

ADULT CHILDREN OF ALCOHOLICS
Janet Woititz

Over a year on *The New York Times* Best-Seller list, this book is the primer on Adult Children of Alcoholics.

ISBN 0-932194-15-X   **$6.95**

STRUGGLE FOR INTIMACY
Janet Woititz

Another best-seller, this book gives insightful advice on learning to love more fully.

ISBN 0-932194-25-7   **$6.95**

BRADSHAW ON: THE FAMILY: A Revolutionary Way of Self-Discovery
John Bradshaw

The host of the nationally televised series of the same name shows us how families can be healed and individuals can realize full potential.

ISBN 0-932194-54-0   **$9.95**

HEALING THE SHAME THAT BINDS YOU
John Bradshaw

This important book shows how toxic shame is the core problem in our compulsions and offers new techniques of recovery vital to all of us.

ISBN 0-932194-86-9   **$9.95**

HEALING THE CHILD WITHIN: Discovery and Recovery for
Adult Children of Dysfunctional Families — Charles Whitfield, M.D.

Dr. Whitfield defines, describes and discovers how we can reach our Child Within to heal and nurture our woundedness.

ISBN 0-932194-40-0   **$8.95**

A GIFT TO MYSELF: A Personal Guide To Healing My Child Within
Charles L. Whitfield, M.D.

Dr. Whitfield provides practical guidelines and methods to work through the pain and confusion of being an Adult Child of a dysfunctional family.

ISBN 1-55874-042-2   **$11.95**

HEALING TOGETHER: A Guide To Intimacy And Recovery For
Co-dependent Couples — Wayne Kritsberg, M.A.

This is a practical book that tells the reader why he or she gets into dysfunctional and painful relationships, and then gives a concrete course of action on how to move the relationship toward health.

ISBN 1-55784-053-8   **$8.95**

3201 S.W. 15th Street,
Deerfield Beach, FL 33442
1-800-851-9100

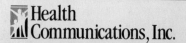 **Health Communications, Inc.**

Helpful 12-Step Books from . . .
Health Communications

12 STEPS TO SELF-PARENTING For Adult Children
Philip Oliver-Diaz, M.S.W., and Patricia A. O'Gorman, Ph.D.

This gentle 12-Step guide takes the reader from pain to healing and self-parenting, from anger to forgiveness, and from fear and despair to recovery.

ISBN 0-932194-68-0 $7.95

SELF-PARENTING 12-STEP WORKBOOK: Windows To Your Inner Child
Patricia O'Gorman, Ph.D., and Philip Oliver-Diaz, M.S.W.

This workbook invites you to become the complete individual you were born to be by using visualizations, exercises and experiences designed to reconnect you to your inner child.

ISBN 1-55874-052-X $9.95

THE 12-STEP STORY BOOKLETS
Mary M. McKee

Each beautifully illustrated booklet deals with a step, using a story from nature in parable form. The 12 booklets (one for each step) lead us to a better understanding of ourselves and our recovery.

ISBN 1-55874-002-3 $8.95

VIOLENT VOICES:
12 Steps To Freedom From Emotional And Verbal Abuse
Kay Porterfield, M.A.

By using the healing model of the 12 Steps emotionally abused women are shown how to deal effectively with verbal and psychological abuse and to begin living as healed and whole people.

ISBN 1-55874-028-7 $9.95

GIFTS FOR PERSONAL GROWTH & RECOVERY
Wayne Kritsberg

A goldmine of positive techniques for recovery (affirmations, journal writing, visualizations, guided meditations, etc.), this book is indispensable for those seeking personal growth.

ISBN 0-932194-60-5 $6.95

3201 S.W. 15th Street,
Deerfield Beach, FL 33442
1-800-851-9100

Health Communications, Inc.